The Art of Agile Living

Conquer Procrastination, Hit Deadlines, Reduce Stress

Helene Gidley and Tom Meloche

The Art of Agile Living

Conquer Procrastination, Hit Deadlines, Reduce Stress

Helene Gidley and Tom Meloche

ISBN 9798324264604

© 2024 Helene Gidley and Tom Meloche

Tweet This Book!

Please help Helene Gidley and Tom Meloche by spreading the word about this book on Twitter!

The suggested tweet for this book is:

I just bought The Art of Agile Living and am looking forward to getting things done!

The suggested hashtag for this book is ##theartofagileliving #gettingthingsdone.

Find out what other people are saying about the book by clicking on this link to search for this hashtag on Twitter:

##theartofagileliving #gettingthingsdone

Contents

Praise for The Art of Agile Living i

The Art of Agile Living™: An Introduction 1

Audience 3

How to Use This Book 5

Special Features and Benefits 7

The Art of Agile Living, An Evolution 9
    A Different Approach to Manage Tasks 12
    The Start of Something New 14

Goodbye, Overwhelm: A Florida Condo and a Visioning
    Ceremony 17
    Things Get Complicated 18
    Agile to the Rescue! and a Trick Called Kanban 18

Working From Home: A New World 21
    A Radically Different World 21
    The Tool That Solves It 22
    The First Giant Leap 23
    Where Did This Idea Come From? 23
    The Art of Agile Living in 7 Steps 24
    Key Takeaways 25

CONTENTS

Step 1: Define Your Work 27
    Here's What You Do: 27
    The Story 27
    And That's Step 1! 28
    Why Physical Paper? 29
    Key Takeaways From Step 1 37

Step 2: Estimate Your Work 39
    Here's What You Do: 39
    The Story 39
    A Great Idea, Gone Bad 40
    I Learned Something Transformative 41
    Why Estimating is So Powerful 42
    How to Do a Solid Estimate 43
    Why Smaller is Better 43
    What My List Looks Like 44
    When is it "Done"? 45
    Prevent Multitasking 45
    When You Delegate, Don't Estimate 46
    It's a Kind of Magic 46
    Key Takeaways From Step 2 47

Step 3: Order Your Work 49
    Here's What You Do: 49
    The Story 49
    So What About All These Sticky Notes? 51
    Two Ways to Organize 53
    Launching the Perfect Monday 55
    Don't Miss Your Big Scheduled Items 56
    The Myth of the 8-Hour Day 58
    Start With Six 58
    Key Takeaways From Step 3 59

Sidebar: Out of Sight, Out of Mind By Bryan Todd 61

Sidebar: The Eisenhower Principle 65

Step 4: Do Your Work 69
    Here's What You Do: 69
    The Story 69
    One Thing, and One Thing Only 71
    Physically Mark It and Move It 74
    Expect Surprises, and Add Them to Your List 74
    Get Your Life Back: Delegate! 75
    Key Takeaways From Step 4 76

Sidebar: A Princess and a Hippopotamus 77

Step 5: Review Your Day 79
    Here's What You Do: 79
    The Principle 79
    Break the Barriers to Completion 80
    How to Finish Out Your Day 84
    Key Takeaways From Step 5 84

Step 6: Update Your Backlog 85
    Here's What You Do: 85
    The Story 85
    Enter the Backlog Planning Sheet 86
    Break it Into Pieces 88
    This is Actually Ideal 88
    And Not Just One Sheet! 89
    Longer Term Items 90
    I Might Want To Do Someday 92
    Still, Beware of Multitasking 93
    Your Weekly Planning Ceremony 94
    Recheck Your Estimates 95
    Go Hippo Hunting 95
    Key Takeaways From Step 6 95

Step 7: List Your Outstanding Items 97
    Here's What You Do: 97
    The Story 97

CONTENTS

When Work Involves Others 98
A Special Note, Just for This 99
Key Takeaways From Step 7 102

Sidebar: The Corkboard Trick By Bryan Todd 103

The Power of Pairing 107
First Element: Keep it Physical 108
Second Element: Make it Social 109
Your Agile "Workout Buddy" 109
Key Takeaways 110

Variations on a Theme: The Art of Agile Living for Family Get-Togethers 111
Agile to the Rescue, Again 112
And Then, a Surprise 114
Watch as the Idea Spreads 115
Key Takeaways 118

The Doorway Effect 121
This is Virtual, Too 122
Your Computer is a Culprit 123
Stickies, Everywhere 124
Keep it Physical, Keep it Safe 124
Key Takeaways 125

The Checklist and the Ceremony 127
Enter the Checklist 128
Without a Ceremony, It's Useless 129
The Crucial Mistake 130
Bring on the Copilot! 131
Choose NOT to Do It 131
Choose to Hand it Off 132
Key Takeaways 133

A Day in the Life 135

> Defining Done 135
> Those Unfinished Tasks 137
> My Daily Ceremony 139
> Dealing with Interrupts 139
> Daily Retrospective 141
> Key takeaways: 142

In Closing: A Solution You Can Stick With 143
> Those Old Abandoned Methods 143
> Designed to Help You Stick to It 144
> You CAN Take it With You 145
> All the Right Motivators 145
> Key Takeaways 146

Resources 149

Acknowledgements 151
> Helene's Acknowledgements 151
> Tom's Acknowledgements 152

About The Authors 153

Praise for The Art of Agile Living

"Many books offering advice on how to take hold of your life simply manage awake feelings of guilt and inadequacy. Not this book. It gently understands your struggles when trying to tame the chaos of the relentless overlapping demands of work and private life. It shows you steps to organize your tasks and life, taking you on a journey from chaos to Kanban. And all you need to take along to this journey is your thorough expertise of what you need to get done, and some post-it notes and pens.

There is something remarkable in the fact that this very tactile low-tech practice to organize your life originates from the software industry. The well-kept secret is that people who gave us online calendars and scheduling systems grab post-it notes and Kanban when organizing their own work. Authors of this book share this secret with you. Their personal stories of taming the chaos in their lives provides enjoyable and encouraging reading."

-Dr. Mari Kira, Assistant Professor of Psychology, University of Michigan.

"A short read packed with practical ideas, The Art of Agile Living, has all the tools you need to get you out of your crazy life and keep you there. Using lessons we've successfully applied on complex software projects at our company for over two decades, Helene Gidley and Tom Meloche teach you how to bring these lessons home and get the whole family participating. Move from overwhelmed to in-control and have fun doing it!"

-Richard Sheridan, CEO & Chief Storyteller, Menlo Innovations

Author, Joy Inc. - How We Built a Workplace People Love and

Praise for The Art of Agile Living

Chief Joy Officer - How Great Leaders Elevate Human Energy and Eliminate Fear

Helene Gidley was one of my early Agile mentors and a collaborator on some of the processes that my team still uses today. When I saw that she had written a book on getting my personal life together, it was something I definitely wanted to get my hands on! In this book, Helene explores the reasons why it's hard to get things done, and then provides tactics that make it simple to translate what we do at work to how we can get things done at home. You don't need software for this – you can just use sticky notes and the side of your refrigerator!

-Megan Torrance, Chief Energy Officer and founder of TorranceLearning Author of Agile for Instructional Designers

"as an Entrepreneur and consultant, one is always looking for ways to increase productivity and simply get stuff done. Whether with your team, your client's or in your own business. The environment is noisy and many claim to have the latest "life hack" . Tom and Helene are among those few that I listen to and whose advice I actually put to use. I was familiar with some of the agile methodology but they have helped me to acquire a deeper understanding of the concepts in PRACTICE. Which as we know is where it matters. I can pretty much guarantee that if you work on actual projects (as opposed to just talking about them) you will get a lot of this latest installment from a trusted source"

-Gabe Bautista, Entrepreneur

"Thanks for sending this to me. It will help me organize my retirement! I love the sticky notes and I will try to incorporate the planning to make my tasks more visible, and hopefully more "complete-able". I tend to get bogged down with my projects because I don't break them into achievable chunks. I'm going to grab a new pack of sticky notes and get to work."

-Lew Stoffel RN, Oncology Certified Nurse (OCN)

"I have a friend that is really struggling with life right now. He is my age and his wife is pregnant (YIKES). And sadly, his house just burned down. I can only imagine that this process would help him keep track of the overwhelming tasks he has to keep up with around the insurance adjusters, the doctors, finding a new place to live, hiring someone to rebuild a house, etc. Can I share a copy with him?"

-Matt Lasater, CEO Engaged Agility (requesting sending an advanced copy to a friend, we said YES :-)

The Art of Agile Living™: An Introduction

Have you ever found yourself up late at night, having to finish a report due the next day ... even though you had known about it weeks before?

Have you ever missed a family dinner or a special personal event, because you spent your entire day running behind and couldn't get caught up?

Have you resolved to start a basic exercise routine, and then watched as it failed to materialize, all because it felt like you could never find the time to fit it in?

If you've experienced any of these frustrations, *this book is for you.*

Embodied in these pages is **The Art of Agile Living™**, a simple yet powerful approach to managing your daily tasks and taking back control of your working life.

Whether it's your job, your home, your family, or your leisure activities, one thing is true: If you want to manage your time, you first have to manage your tasks. That's the holy grail. The Art of Agile Living is a method for doing just that. It's a simple, physical, tactile approach that creates anticipation around your work and a tangible feeling of reward for each task you get done.

And yet this book is not about tasks. It's not about sticky notes or sheets of paper. It's not about checklists. It is about the power you'll find in a simple ritual—a ceremony—for structuring and planning each day. A ritual that will become so much of a beloved habit that you'll never again want to start a day without it.

And not just any one day. The Art of Agile Living helps you retake control over your entire week. Over all your biggest projects.

Imagine: everything you've been itching to get done, everything connected to your work, your home, your family, your recreation, your social activities—all contained in one place. Easy to manage, every single item planned and scheduled, so that you're able to give each task your 100% focus, free of worry and distraction.

Projects that may have been sitting untouched for days, weeks, months, even years—finally finished and done.

Agile is an idea conceived years ago in the software development industry. People there felt constantly overwhelmed by the work; exhausted teams watched as expensive projects went past deadline and over budget again and again. Agile was created as a solution, and revolutionized the way software projects are done.

From that inspiration we've created The Art of Agile Living, where we take the very best from that industry and give you an easy-to-implement daily practice. We'll show you an empirical approach that serves you no matter your field of work, all based on Agile's core principles of simplicity, transparency, and focus.

Whether you're an employee working from home, an entrepreneur, a student, or a stay-at-home parent or grandparent, you'll benefit from the clarity and focus it gives you. You'll find The Art of Agile Living to be an invaluable tool for managing your time—and your life—effectively.

Audience

This chapter is dedicated to those grappling with the intricate dance of managing both personal and professional responsibilities. In particular, we address two standout groups: the driven and ambitious Entrepreneurs and small business owners, along with the fast-paced world of busy business professionals.

For Entrepreneurs and small business owners, the challenges are uniquely daunting, as they navigate a multitude of roles within their ventures. The Art of Agile Living offers a systematic approach to handling tasks and responsibilities, providing a pathway to boost productivity and attain goals efficiently. The flexibility inherent in your work processes allows for seamless integration of the strategies outlined in The Art of Agile Living, facilitating a harmonious balance between personal and professional spheres.

Meanwhile, busy business professionals entrenched in high-pressure environments are no strangers to the perpetual struggle of harmonizing demanding work schedules with personal lives. If you find yourself in this category, constantly on the lookout for effective time management strategies, The Art of Agile Living steps in as a practical solution. This framework offers structure and adaptability, guiding you in organizing your workload and maintaining focus on priorities. By embracing the strategies embedded in The Art of Agile Living, professionals like you can witness heightened productivity and a regained sense of control over the delicate interplay of work and personal life.

How to Use This Book

This book walks you through the evolution and background of The Art of Agile Living process, giving you a thorough understanding of not only how to use the process, but why it is so powerful. We recommend reading the book in its entirety. We realize, however, that you may want to skip through to specific sections.

If you're looking for an overview of the process, read the Working From Home chapter.

If you want to skip right to learning how to utilize the seven steps of The Art of Agile Living process, read the sections Define Your Work through List Your Outstanding Items.

For some excellent examples of variations of this process, read the Family Gatherings section.

The A Day In The Life chapter provides an excellent example of using The Art of Agile Living process over the course of one day.

Special Features and Benefits

Easy-to-Follow Steps: Simple, practical step-by-step instructions make it easy for readers to implement agile techniques in their daily lives.

Real-Life Examples: Filled with relatable anecdotes and real-life examples, demonstrating how agile principles can be applied in various situations and scenarios.

Flexible Alternatives: Presenting a range of alternative approaches, providing flexibility and customization to suit each individual's unique needs and preferences.

Online Video Support: Complemented by a series of online videos featuring the authors, providing additional insights and demonstrating the application of agile living techniques in real-life situations. Available on our YouTube channel at www.youtube.com/@a2agile.

The Art of Agile Living, An Evolution

The spark that created The Art of Agile Living

I've always worked with some kind of to-do list. Early in my career the to-do items weren't that lengthy, and I could keep most of the items in my head. That was well before the intrusion of the digital aids of laptops, cell phones, iPads, and smart watches. All these items that were meant to make our lives easier.

As a Project Manager in the Information Technology area I always had large to-do lists. Over time as the lists got ever longer I looked to other means to organize my workload. Things like the DayTimer® system of tracking project items on separate to-do lists that can fit into your jacket pocket. Handy little sheets of paper no wider than a mens shirt pocket. Separate sheets of paper for project lists, separate sheets for project specific to-do lists, separate sheets for goals, and so on. All meant to be portable, easily carried between meetings. Over time I found the plethora of separate sheets distracting. While it tried to create focus, having so many sheets for so many things left me unfocused.

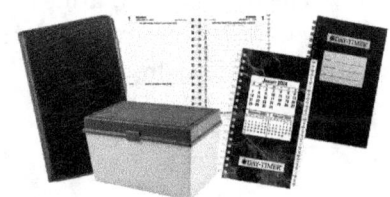

I tried the FranklinPlanner© approach. With its notebook format, daily planning sheets, and separate tabs for each month. Portability was key with the notebook format, making it easy to carry to meetings. The ability to add extra sheets to the notebook for taking notes based on each project helped consolidate information on each project. However, each to-do list was still scattered across the multiple tabs and became more project focused. I wound up morphing the Franklin Planner to be a tabbed notebook, where I kept notes on each project, but not the to-do lists. Those I continued to struggle with.

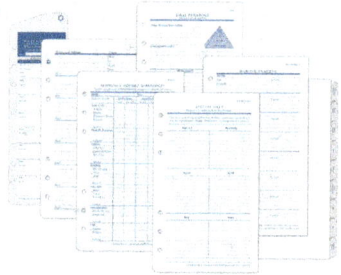

These are each worthy tools. Yet despite their simple, tactile approach, I was still unable to effectively manage my workload.

Likewise, I found low motivation for getting anything done when faced with a large to-do list. Frozen, like a deer in the headlights. That's what the large list of things felt like. The list of things that needed to be done now, things to be done soon, and some that are to be done later. All jumbled together. Staring at me. Unmovable. Unrelenting. Always there. Like the stunned deer, I felt sure to be run over by the sheer weight of my to-do list.

And so nothing gets done.

Until I was introduced to a unique method of planning work. On physical sheets of paper, that was being used for planning work for large Information Technology projects. Each piece of work was folded into a size that represented how long it would take to complete. Sizes like half-week, full week, two weeks. These were placed onto large planning sheets that represented two weeks of an Information Technology developer. In one simple step, two week's worth of time was scheduled. Best yet, the time could not be over-scheduled since only a finite amount of sized tasks could fit on the planning sheet. In one simple step the work to be done was ordered from the most important to least important. In one simple step the work became focused. In one simple step no one felt like a deer in the headlights.

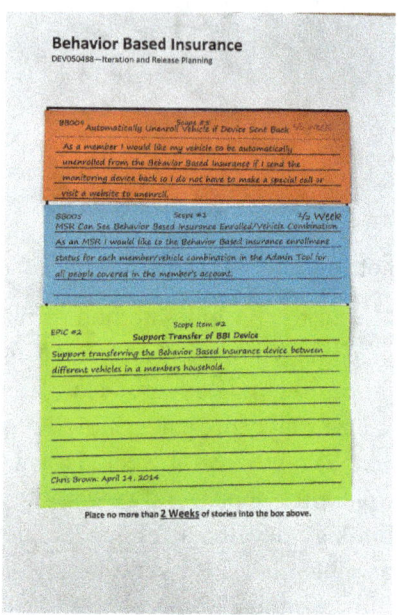

In one simple step *work got done*.

This was the beauty and magic of an agile approach. Born from the Information Technology field, used to manage large, complex projects. Teams of developers were using this method to manage their tasks and get things done. Something about this was wildly appealing to me and my challenge of managing my daily tasks.

A Different Approach to Manage Tasks

A few years later I was working with another Project Manager on similar projects. We agreed to help support each other and back each other up. We both had the same experience in managing project tasks with the folded paper on 11 x 17 planning sheets. To better manage our own project management tasks, we decided to try this method. We wrote our tasks on paper, folded them to represent the amount of time they would take to complete, and placed them on our own 11 x 17 daily planning sheets. Our sheets represented one 8-hour day of our time. We were very proud of our planning approach. Suddenly our work was focused. Our day was well planned. Everything seemed to fit perfectly. Surely everything would get done as planned with such an elegant process in place.

Unfortunately our first pass at this was a failure.

We neglected the fact that scheduled meetings actually take time away from your day for getting tasks done. We didn't think to place them on our daily planning sheet. Once we did, we gained great insight into what constitutes a productive day. The concept of the 8-hour day myth was born. Once we began planning out our estimated and folded days tasks onto a 11x17 sheet of paper representing an 8 hour day, and added our planned meetings, we quickly realized that 8 hours of tasks do not fit. And once we added time for phone calls, interruptions from colleagues, emails, and even bathroom breaks, we realized that 6 hours of time to work on tasks was the best we could plan for.

So we adjusted our planning sheets. We included the meetings. We adjusted our day to be no more than 6 hours long. We planned our days based on the shorter available time. We gave this adjusted plan a try.

It worked.

Best of all, we were beginning to get our work done on time, regularly. We were prepared for meetings. Our status reports were not late. We no longer had to work overtime to get the basics done. When managers and colleagues asked for new tasks to be done, we could effectively answer when that new piece of work would be completed. We had a system for handling our work. It was a game changer for us.

My personal tasks however, continued to be a list of to-do items. A list that felt manageable. For a while anyway.

Fast forward a decade, and the amount of personal work competing for my time has increased almost tenfold. My to-do lists could no longer keep pace with the increased amount of personal and job-related tasks. My experience with agile teams was teaching me the value of breaking work into small chunks to get more done. Scheduling work for agile teams was focused on weekly or bi-weekly plans. Focused, planned work for short time frames. This worked for complex IT projects. Why couldn't this work for my personal tasks?

The Start of Something New

Following the principles and practices of agile for software development, I broke down all my work, personal and professional, into small chunks. I estimated them. I ordered them based on importance. I made sure to include hard demands on my time (having learned my lesson from my project manager 11x17 task sheet). I put them on a single sheet of paper representing a day of work. I was sure to not schedule more than 6 hours of tasks. I focused on only one task at a time.

This worked nicely for a single day. I was focused and had a well structured plan for the day. It felt very reassuring and calming.

But what about all the rest of the to-do items that won't get done today? Having them in a big pile on my desk was not very effective or conducive to getting anything done. It again felt like that big to-do list. Ever growing, ever imposing, ever stifling. Borrowing again from the agile practices, I extended my planning to include the 5-day workweek. One sheet for every day of the week so I could begin to plan out my entire week. One sheet for the items that won't get done this week, but need to be on my radar so I don't forget about them. Suddenly I had a system for handling not only my personal tasks, but my work related tasks. All in one place.

It worked right from the start.

Borrowing from my many years as a Project Management Professional, I included ways to keep track of things I'm waiting on from others. And when my weekends felt just as busy, well, I added a sheet of paper for handling my weekend tasks.

The Art of Agile Living was born. A daily practice to keep you focused and calm. A daily practice to keep you from being that deer in the headlights, unable to move from the weight of all the work weighing you down.

This book is to share my practice with you. To give you a simple and practical method to manage the huge number of tasks coming your way. To share options and variations that may work better for you. To let you manage your overwhelm.

Goodbye, Overwhelm: A Florida Condo and a Visioning Ceremony

My husband David and I have been friends with another couple, Glen and Karen, since 2007. In fact, David and Glen were college roommates in the 1970s, so they go back even further. Since 2007 the four of us have become best of friends; we've traveled overseas together and we even have vacation residences in the same condominium complex in Florida.

Something has always struck me about Glen and Karen: They have amazing methods for managing processes and work. They bring terrific organizational skills and clear thinking to everything they do.

I've enjoyed a firsthand view of this over the years. Glen keeps a spreadsheet that lists every paint color on every wall of their Florida condo. Karen uses a detailed city-by-city travel folder when she plans international trips. They are superb at managing complex situations.

A couple of years ago, they were faced with a decision: Do they sell their Florida condo and consolidate their homes?

To help with decisions like this, I have some tools and skills of my own. One of them is something I call a Visioning Ceremony.

I walked them through pros and cons. We broke all the various options down into categories. We gave each option a relative weight. We ran through scenarios for each option.

Every one of Glen's and Karen's individual views and opinions was represented, honored, and explored. We got every last piece of crucial information out in the open, so that they could see it, discuss it, and reach a conclusion together.

And here's an essential detail: I mapped out all of this with them *there, in the room, on a physical wall.* With sticky notes. Lots and lots of sticky notes!

It turns out their final decision was to sell their Florida condo. Sad for David and me, but clearly the right move for them.

Things Get Complicated

Years earlier we had offered to purchase their condo if they ever sold. And that's exactly what happened. We launched into the project of doing just that. And a complex project it was!

Karen found herself faced with a multitude of tasks: moving furniture and valuables from Florida to Michigan; organizing donations; cleaning out fourteen years of accumulated stuff; managing a roof fix and a screen installation; and more. All of this while still receiving house guests! (Vacation homes are prone to frequent family visits.)

With a project of this complexity, even Karen found her superhero organizational skills overwhelmed.

Agile to the Rescue! and a Trick Called Kanban

But to my surprise and elation, Karen had borrowed a method she had seen me use many times: She wrote out all her essential tasks on sticky notes. She organized them and placed them on a sliding glass door, there in the open, for her and Glen and everyone else to see and work with. Columns titled: D&H, Donate, MI, Storage, and departure timings. With sticky notes like: Foyer desk, living room couch, etc. Each sticky note indicating items specific to each column.

A method I had used for years for myself and clients she had now adopted in order to manage the sale of her Florida vacation home and the big move back to Michigan.

What she didn't realize is that she had created her own kanban[1] board—without ever knowing what kanban was; no training class,

---

[1] Originally developed by Taiichi Ohno, an industrial engineer at Toyota, to improve manufacturing efficiency, kanban is a method of defining and visualizing work to improve workflow.

no podcast, no book guiding her. Just her implementing something she had seen me do countless times.

And this simple technique *solved her overwhelm!*

Few things in life are more rewarding than seeing your favorite techniques adopted, adapted, and used by others. It's our delight to do exactly that, for you.

In this book we'll teach you how to use kanban to do The Art of Agile Living. You can apply these methods to your professional and personal work. The results will surprise and delight you.

Working From Home: A New World

The world changed forever in 2020. The COVID-19 pandemic sent millions of people to work at home for the very first time. And if you're like me, you watched your work life and home life blend and blur like never before.

One direct effect was that you saw your daily task list grow and multiply. Far more than you planned on. Now that you were at home, every time you got up from your work desk and headed to the kitchen for a cup of coffee you saw something else that needed to be done: mail to open, bills to pay, toys to pick up, and a dog to walk. You noticed that the vase was dusty and the carpet a bit of a mess. You saw out the window that the grass had grown and needed mowing.

Your list grew as a mounting jumble of fuzzy responsibilities accumulating in your mind. You arrived back from your coffee break not refreshed or relaxed but overwhelmed, as you registered a new pile of to-dos. And then you sat down at your desk to find that your email inbox had received nine new messages.

Familiar?

How can you stay on top of all this and not let critical items fall through the cracks? How do you manage your work without feeling overwhelmed, giving up, and turning on Netflix?

A Radically Different World

In 1981 I worked for a Fortune 500 company in New Jersey. Steeped in the IT field as a mainframe Systems Programmer, I spent all day on a computer terminal interacting with others and the mainframe, writing programs, debugging errors, installing software.

What a radically different world that was.

When I was at work, I was totally immersed in it. Apart from the rare occasions that our team needed to put in extra hours or come in on weekends, once I went home for the day, *I left work behind.* There was little to no blending of work and home life. Like everyone else, I had no cell phone sitting on my person and no laptop computer I carried around.

My significant others, parents, friends, schoolteachers, and doctors could certainly reach me, but not 24/7. The office could only contact me if I was near my landline.

In that environment I had little trouble getting things done, whether work tasks or home tasks. Interruptions at work were work related; interruptions at home were home related.

Wherever I was, I could be present in the moment. I could focus on the single issue or task I had at hand.

Today our work and professional lives constantly intermingle. Communications have enabled us to be connected through devices we carry and wear. The cacophony of email, Slack, text messages, work requests, news, and teleconferences can be deafening. Add to this the fact that so many of us are now working from home, and the to-do list in our heads grows exponentially. How do we manage life's daily chaos?

That's what we're here to help you answer.

The Tool That Solves It

Our goal is to help you prevent all-nighters and last-minute panics. For you to freely take action on all the tasks and responsibilities that your work life *and* home life require ... and to be able to "leave work behind" at the end of each day.

Kanban is our tool. It's the centerpiece of everything we'll teach you, a physical process that works by getting the overwhelm out of your head and onto paper.

And to make kanban work, we'll show you seven simple steps you can follow every day to complete your tasks and keep overwhelm far, far away.

These steps serve your professional work, as well as any and all other big activities like moving, throwing a party, remodeling, and more. Any large task you're doing that feels overwhelming, you can reduce and simplify with this method.

The First Giant Leap

We've already mentioned that kanban involves sticky notes. Lots of them.

That's because the first giant leap toward eliminating overwhelm is to take all the abstract, conceptual work ideas swimming in our heads and turn them into something concrete.

Specifically: *Get every last to-do out of your head and onto paper.*

That's what the sticky notes do. Once you have your tasks written out on separate pieces of paper, you can now manipulate them as a physical thing. Something finite that you can see, touch, focus on, and then mark as complete and set aside once you're done.

Where Did This Idea Come From?

Kanban is a scheduling system that originated in the world of manufacturing. It's a method to manage the flow of work in systems.

The Art of Agile Living is particularly effective because it takes kanban and marries it with all the learning styles: visual, auditory, kinesthetic; reading and writing.

These differing styles drive not only our approach to learning, but how we process and internalize new information. There are lots of benefits:

- Writing our work down allows us to stop over-relying on our memory.
- Writing it down appeals to writing and reading learning styles.
- Making it visible appeals to those who thrive on visual cues.
- By working with paper, we engage kinesthetic learning.

The Art of Agile Living in 7 Steps

I've known and used Agile techniques for decades, and I've been applying them to my at-home tasks for over ten years. The process is incredibly easy to implement. Once you become familiar with it, you'll barely notice the steps.

An Agile workday goes like this:

Step 1: Define Your Work

Step 2: Estimate Your Work

Step 3: Order Your Work

Step 4: Do Your Work

Step 5: Review Your Day

Step 6: Update Your Backlog

Step 7: List Your Outstanding Items

Through the rest of this book we'll walk you through the steps one at a time. You'll see exactly what The Art of Agile Living looks like as part of the process, and how to use it to eliminate your overwhelm.

Key Takeaways

- The line between home life and work life is easily blurred, and needs extra attention and special skills to manage.
- Kanban originated in manufacturing, but it has value in nearly every working environment you can imagine.
- You'll find a giant leap forward simply in getting every task out of your head and onto physical paper.
- Work becomes so much easier when you can enhance your focus and stay present in the moment.

Step 1: Define Your Work

Turning your abstract ideas into concrete, motivated actions

Here's What You Do:

- Every item you can think of that needs to be done, write a physical sticky note for it: work tasks, home tasks, personal life tasks.
- For each task, use a separate 1.5 x 2-inch Post-It™ Note.
- Spend 5-10 minutes at the beginning of every day breaking down existing work into the exact tasks you need to get done today.

The Story

We arrived at our newly purchased Florida condominium in January. It was our winter getaway, and I was instantly inundated with a plethora of tasks: unpacking, organizing, finding artwork for our empty walls, coming up with decorating ideas, transferring prescriptions to our Florida pharmacy, and more.

There were so many small items running around in my head that I feared I would forget the big ones, like paying the bills.

Thankfully, I have a method for just this situation. I grabbed my pad of sticky notes. Every item I could think of, I wrote a sticky note for it. These sticky notes include "Unpack 3 Bins", "Organize Coffee Supplies in Kitchen", "Pay Credit Card Bill".

Step 1: Define Your Work

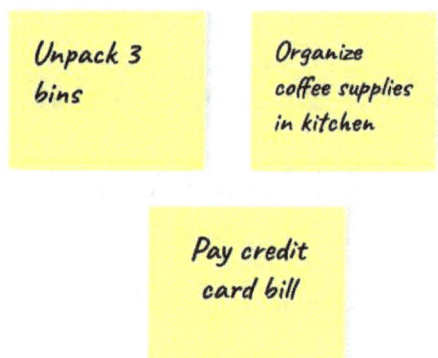

When I write something down, I know I won't forget it. When it's on a physical piece of paper, I know I can manage it.

And That's Step 1!

Start by simply listing "The Work" that you need to do. All of it. Or at least as much as you can remember right now. Don't worry about the other stuff you know you're forgetting; our process will allow you to catch later anything you may not think of at the moment.

The Work includes tasks from your employer, your list of tasks from home, and any other tasks you may create or have in mind that will help you achieve your personal goals and ambitions. That list exists somewhere—most likely in your head.

Tasks may include paying bills, doing laundry, washing your car, painting the garage, and completing that status report due to your boss. Account for everything you have in your head right now that you know you need to do—anything you might worry about forgetting or leaving undone. In my case I even include items such as exercise.

Why bother writing all this down? You might think that since you already know everything that needs to be done you don't need to put it into writing. But it's a safe bet you've been operating that way for years now, and the reason you're reading this is because something about it isn't working. Perhaps you've found that items get lost, tasks never get done, or you spend too many late nights in a frantic panic to get caught up before a big deadline.

You write things down because *out of sight is out of mind.* And work that is "out of mind" can be easily forgotten or preempted by trivial momentary distractions. Writing things down is the first step toward managing the work rather than letting the work manage you.

We recommend a very specific method:

1. Use physical paper.
2. For each task, use a separate 1.5 x 2-inch Post-It™ Note.

Why Physical Paper?

Writing things on paper, in a physical format where you can easily move it around, forces you to become more connected to the work. And more connected means more mindful, more present, and more focused on *what needs to get done in the moment.*

Yes, the physical action of holding and manipulating paper does exactly this. It gives you a physical item to interact with and manage. What was initially an abstract idea is now a visual, concrete item in actual space. Something you and anyone else can see and touch and feel.

Why Sticky Notes?

Sticky notes fit neatly onto a regular piece of paper. They let you divide the work into separate, discrete tasks that you can easily move about and rearrange. You can take any single task and edit it, reword it, replace it, or mark it as done. (More on this later.)

We love this approach because it incorporates both visual and kinesthetic learning styles.

What is kinesthetics, and why is it so important?

Of all the five senses, sight, smell, hearing, taste, and touch, the sense of touch stands out as unique. Unique in that it is the one sense that we initiate. To experience the sense of touch, we actively cause ourselves to engage in touch. We actively move our muscles to reach the item we are interested in, and further move our muscles to engage in actually touching the item. Eyesight, hearing, smell, and even taste all happen to us. Light is directed towards our eyes, captured on the retina, and converted to an image. All without our having to initiate anything other than opening our eyelids. Similarly, we may put something in our mouths, but the taste buds activate on their own to give us the sense of taste. For us to experience touch, we actively engage our muscles.

This recognition of actively engaging the sense of touch, making it unique amongst the senses, has been a source of study for centuries. In 1812 Xavier Bichet felt this initiation of touch by the organism itself makes touch different from and fundamental to the other senses[1]. No other sense requires us to take such an active role. In 1749 David Hartley held the belief that the sense of touch, which he felt was a combination of pressure and muscular contraction, gave rise to knowledge of material objects. Not even eyesight was as a reliable source of the knowledge of material objects over the sense of touch, according to Hartley. It was only the sense of touch that

---

[1]Bichat, Xavier, Anatomie générale, appliquée a la physiologie et a la médecine, 2nd edn, 4 vols (Paris 1812) [first publ. 1801] vol. 1, 117

provided the essential properties of matter[2].

Widely held theories during the nineteenth century stipulated that touch provided knowledge of ourselves and the world. It was postulated that touch brought about a sense of us separate from the world, and that spatial recognition emanated from muscular sensation[3]. These ideas show that many in the medical field felt that the sense of touch was unique and special. Being called various things, from terms including muscular contraction, pressure, to vibrations, it was Charles Bell in 1833 to first describe the sense of touch as a Sixth Sense[4] . Bell asserts that this Sixth Sense is the consciousness of exertion, a muscular sense. One of two required for the sensation of touch. The other being muscular action. He believed that there existed a circular path amongst the nerves and brain. The nerves that contract muscles for motion and those that provide the sensation of movement. Through his experimentation he believed that these nerves could only carry one type of information - either motion or the sensation of motion[5].

The focus of early twentieth century research into movement of the body, exercise and movement for general improvements of health, saw the adoption of the kinesthetic term. The term "Kinesthetic" describes the complex of sensations that are part of this sixth sense—very simply, our sensory perception of movement.[6] From the early research, we can still take away the realization that the sense of touch is foundational to our understanding of material objects. Touch has a two-way street to the brain, both in muscular movement and in transmitting the actual sensory information. Engaging touch in what we do has a direct connection to our brain.

---

[2]Hartley, David, Observations on Man, His Frame, His Duty, and His Expectations, 2 vols (London 1749)

[3]Wundt, Wilhelm, Grundzüge der physiologischen Psychologie (Leipzig 1874)

[4]It should be noted that there are two uses of the term Sixth Sense, one being more of an intuition or mystical nature, and one being more sensory knowledge. It is the sensory knowledge use of the Sixth Sense that we refer to in this book.

[5]Bell, Charles, The Hand: Its Mechanism and Vital Endowments as Evincing Design, 2nd edn (London 1833) [first publ. 1833]

[6]H. C Bastian The "muscular sense"; its nature and cortical localisation. Brain 10: 1-8,1887. - reference removed

Today, the definition of kinesthetics hasn't changed much from it's initial use. The dictionary defines kinesthetic as a sense mediated by receptors located in muscles, tendons, and joints and stimulated by bodily movements and tensions[7]. That sense of touch, and its connection to the brain and the understanding of material objects, is the key success factor of the Art of Agile Living practice. By touching the sticky note we recognize it as a material object. By writing the task or idea down on the sticky note, we give rise to the idea moving from something conceptual to something concrete, a material object. Moving the sticky notes on our planning sheets further solidifies the task as now something real, concrete, and physical.

We've engaged our key sense, the sense of touch, into our planning. We're engaging our brains in a deeper, more intentional manner, in our task management. Our tasks are now something far more real than electrons on a screen. To make tasks real and tangible, you and I need to handle them physically. The sticky note has become the task. And moving the task from TO DO to DONE, generates the satisfaction of completion.

Humans have been here for hundreds of thousands of years. We've spent virtually all of that time physically manipulating the world around us. We evolved to see, to feel, and to move things about in physical space.

When you write down tasks and then manage them as a physical thing, you have a constant tangible representation of your progress. When a task is done, you can physically move it to DONE.

The satisfaction of completion is an endorphin rush to the brain. A kick of energy. A warm glow of self-worth.

Best of all, the act of touching each item is also a stimulant for your mind, a repeated mental boost to keep you going. This is "Brain candy" at its best!

---

[7] https://www.merriam-webster.com/dictionary/kinesthetic

So Do This, Now

Take a piece of paper and a set of sticky notes and spend the next few minutes writing down every item on your mental to-do list. Anything undone that's weighing you down, anything rattling around in your head that you need finished. Work tasks, home tasks, personal life tasks; anything. Write it all down, one single item per sticky note. You might end up with more than twenty notes. Or more than sixty! It's all fine.

Do it now. I'll wait.

No, really, do it now!

Finished?

I did this myself as well. My first note says, "Status report." My second note is "Summer camp" and my third note is "Email." These aren't very detailed, but they're the first seeds of thoughts I'm having about what needs to get done. I could leave them in this form, but I might forget what it is I want accomplished with each one. So I'll add more, or possibly rewrite a couple of them, later on.

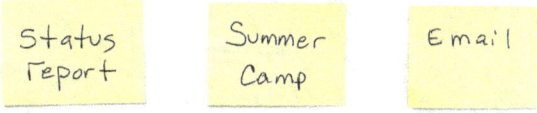

For now, it's fine to write out several short notes like these, just to get your brain started. Sticky notes with "Status Report", "Summer Camp", and "Email".

I'm looking at my sticky note that says, "Status report." It has me thinking ... this is a work item I usually do over several days, but I'd like to identify a single piece of it that I can finish today. I can break up my "Status report" item into three separate notes and add detail to each one.

So I did just that. My first note now reads: "Status report first draft. Bullett list items I don't have material for yet".

> *Status report 1st draft. Bullet list items I don't have material for yet*

This gives me at least one note, one item that I'm confident I can complete today: the first draft of the report.

Breaking work like this into smaller chunks lets me focus on one thing at a time and never get overwhelmed with the size of a project. Working on those smaller chunks and then revisiting the larger task also gives me time to think about the work and uncover missing items.

As I break apart the tasks, I write more on each note to help me remember in the future what exactly it is I want done. So my second note reads: "Status report second draft. Fill in bullet items."

> *Status report 2nd draft. Fill in bullet items.*

And the third reads "Final status report. Proofread. Spell Check. Hand in."

> Final status report. Proofread. Spell Check. Hand in.

I can still rewrite these notes in the future but this is good enough for now.

While creating my first draft I realize that I need to present some of the information in the form of a chart. Aha! I've just uncovered another key piece of work for the report. So I write a new note that says, "Create chart of outstanding tasks for Status Report."

> Create chart of outstanding tasks for Status Report

I discovered this early in the process, which means I have time to address it before the report is due. That's a key trick for avoiding last-minute chaos: write down new work as soon as you discover it.

Any time I find myself getting overwhelmed with a task, or letting it sit undone, I break the task into smaller pieces.

My "Email" sticky note was also too big, and perhaps too vague, so I split it into smaller tasks with better descriptions. Three, to be exact: "Scan through my email and delete any that can be deleted.", "Identify top 2 or 3 email items that need immediate attention and respond.", and "Scan through email and sort messages by project and put in holding folder for action.".

> Scan through my email and delete any that can be deleted

> Identify top 2 or 3 email items that need immediate attention and respond

> Scan through email and sort messages by project and put in holding folder for action

I don't have to work through all my emails in one sitting. Some messages take longer to read, analyze, and act upon. It's because of this uncertainty that I split "Email" into separate tasks.

On my coffee break, after writing these notes, I notice three things to do around the house, "Dust dining room", "Mow Lawn", and "Fix broken lamp" So I write them down when I get back:

I now have three new sticky notes! Any time I think of something new that needs doing, I create a note for it. And yes, I keep a spare pad of sticky notes in nearly every room of the house.

After rewriting some of my notes, and thinking up new ones, I have a nice pile.

Looking at a collection of thirteen sticky notes may feel like a lot, but don't despair. This is just the first step toward chaos management.

I spend five to ten minutes at the beginning of every day breaking down existing tasks and capturing new work. Once you get into a familiar rhythm, this doesn't take long.

Key Takeaways From Step 1

- Make all your work defined and visible.
- Writeced all your tasks to prevent them from becoming "out of sight, out of mind" and being left undone.
- Turn your abstract ideas into concrete, motivated actions using "kinesthetics."
- Break complex work down into smaller, outcome-oriented tasks with clear definitions.

Step 2: Estimate Your Work

Be crystal clear about what "done" means for each task

Here's What You Do:

- For each task, write down a time estimate of how many hours and minutes it will take you, working uninterrupted, to complete it.
- Be crystal clear about what "done" means for each task.
- Keep tasks small; your estimates should be no less than 5 minutes and no more than 2 hours.
- Only estimate the work you do yourself, not what you delegate to others.

The Story

I started making face masks when the Covid-19 pandemic hit. When experts started recommending them but supplies were short, I pulled out whatever elastic and fabric I had around, dusted off the old sewing machine, and started cranking out fabric face masks by hand.

Over time I updated my pattern and process. It became my hobby, and I would gladly spend a couple of hours each evening working on it. I made custom masks for spring, summer, fall, Halloween, and Christmas, and I did collegiate-themed masks for family and friends.

Because it was a hobby, I realized that I hadn't been paying much attention to my actual process.

As much as I enjoyed the work, there were some steps in the sewing sequence that always seemed inefficient and tedious. Specifically, switching out thread colors and laying out patterns for cutting.

A Great Idea, Gone Bad

So I started doing these steps together in bulk, just to get it over with. My thought was that I could more quickly assemble a large number of finished masks at the very end.

While that may seem reasonable, to someone who knows Agile it should sound very wrong.

This became evident to me one particular evening. I had friends coming to town the following day, so I planned to make them three masks each, plus a bandana scarf for their dog, all in University of Michigan colors.

I dove into the work as usual. After a stretch of time I looked at the clock and realized that I had spent two hours and had not produced a single completed mask. Not one. I had a bunch of fabric pieces sitting around, in various stages of assembly, but nothing ready to give away.

What I had created was a process for producing large amounts of *unfinished* pieces of masks. More critically, I had no idea how long it actually took to complete a single mask, start to finish. I had been lured by the temptation of small immediate wins, and had missed the larger goal.

I Learned Something Transformative

So I hit the reset button. The following morning, before my friends arrived, I immediately began working from beginning to end on a single mask. Cutting the fabric, sewing the pieces together, changing the needle and bobbin thread as needed, to get a single mask done.

It turned out that the time required to put together a completed mask was thirty minutes. That's far better than investing two hours' work with no finished product to show for it.

This observation was frankly transformative. Up until now I had been unclear on how long it took to complete a single mask. Not anymore.

That simple thirty-minute span became the guide for all my mask production. When I would sit down for a fixed block of time, I knew exactly how many masks I could complete. And if I had a set number of masks I needed to finish, I knew exactly how many hours and minutes it would take.

This has become a valuable principle that applies to all my work. It keeps me from overcommitting. I can plan ahead and estimate sensibly. If I do it right, I'll never have to stay up late to complete a project by a deadline.

Why Estimating is So Powerful

When I have clear estimates for all my work, I know exactly how to schedule my tasks so that I complete each one.

And watching things *actually get done* is a huge hack for human motivation. It's central to the The Art of Agile Living system.

These lessons apply to every single task I write. For example, today I wrote a note that says "Scan through my email and delete any that can be deleted." I think about this task and I estimate that it might take me just five minutes to complete it. So I write "5 minutes" at the bottom of the note.

> Scan through my
> email and delete
> any that can be
> deleted
> (5 minutes)

When I look over my tasks and I see that this takes only five minutes to complete, I'm far more likely to dive into it. In other words, simply having a clear estimate keeps me from procrastinating.

How to Do a Solid Estimate

This approach has worked well for me: Estimate the time it will take for me, working uninterrupted, to complete the task. Express it in hours and minutes. The smallest estimate I'll ever use is five minutes; the largest is two hours. If a task is longer than two hours I'll break it down into more manageable chunks.

Why the two-hour limit?

Think about your typical workday. Do you ever get more than two hours of time, uninterrupted, where you can focus on completing a single task? For most of us, getting even one hour of focused, uninterrupted time is hard. I've found that anything larger than two hours simply won't get done.

Why Smaller is Better

This leads me to something I think is vitally important: I really, *really* want you to keep your tasks small.

Keeping the tasks as small as possible gives you more flexibility. You can add or remove as many as you need in order to fit each day's schedule. You'll appreciate that when you have extra busy workdays with multiple demands on your time.

More specifically, you'll appreciate the ability to *complete* those tasks. That adds to your motivation. Getting one task done is infinitely more motivating than getting twenty started but not completed. It gives you a greater sense of control over your day. Which means you're more likely to stick to this process.

And that in turn means more time to be with your family, more freedom to enjoy your hobbies, and the ability to get all the sleep you need. You'll be happier for it.

What My List Looks Like

My to-do items now include written estimates ranging from five minutes to two hours each. This includes both home and work tasks. My "Dust dining room" task has an estimate of thirty minutes and my "Mow Lawn" task has an estimate of two hours.

I want to be able to see all my daily tasks for both work and home, with estimates under each one:

Dust dining room (30 minutes)	Schedule my and my daughters dentist appointment so we are on the same day (15 minutes)	Schedule sons dental cleaning appointment Give to husband	Status report 1st draft. Bullet list items I don't have material for yet (1 hour)	Status report 2nd draft. Fill in bullet items. (1 hour)
Final status report. Proofread. Spell Check. Hand in. (1 hour)	Scan through my email and delete any that can be deleted (5 minutes)	Identify top 2 or 3 email items that need immediate attention and respond (15 minutes)	Scan through email and sort messages by project and put in holding folder for action (15 minutes)	MOW LAWN (2 hours)
	Fix Broken Lamp, rewire and add new harp, bulb (2 hours)	Research Summer camps and ID 3 that may be interesting for kids (1 hour)	Create chart of outstanding tasks for status report (45 minutes)	

(What if you have a day-long activity, like a training class or offsite meeting? That would break my two-hour-maximum rule. And that's fine; in this case I'm not dogmatic. I'll allow these activities more than a two-hour time estimate.)

When is it "Done"?

Note that I added a bit more detail to a few of the items when I came up with their estimates. For example, I gave a bit more thought to what's actually involved in fixing a broken lamp. That allowed me to come up with a more accurate time estimate. I rewrote the task as "Fix broken lamp, rewire and add new harp, bulb."

In Agile we call this "being clear about what done means." How exactly do you know when a task is done? Be specific. Write it out.

Prevent Multitasking

You want to avoid having tasks that are never quite done, that sit on your board or wall marked as "ongoing." That leads to multitasking.

And multitasking divides your mind, divides your energy, and leads to huge amounts of wasted time.

And in my case while making face masks, it led to large piles of unfinished work sitting scattered about the room and house.

Our aim is to get control over our work, to be able to mark each task as done within a finite amount of time. The last thing we want is wasted time and divided energy.

More on the perils of multitasking in a later chapter.

When You Delegate, Don't Estimate

As I was estimating my tasks, I noticed that one item could be delegated: "Schedule son's dental cleaning appointment." Since my husband usually schedules our son's dental appointments to coincide with his, I let him handle the task.

And you'll notice I didn't include a time estimate for that one. That's for him to do.

My golden rule of estimating is to only estimate the work I do, not what someone else does. Let people estimate their own work; that allows them to own the task and the process of thinking through what's being asked of them.

It's a Kind of Magic

There is something unique and special about estimating your work as you sit down to write out your day's tasks. It clarifies exactly what you need to do to complete each item, and how long it will take. You re-insert reality into your planning. Reality becomes a motivator.

That's the magic of estimates. They motivate us. Whatever inherent behavior quirks you and I bring to our work, this method allows us to move past them.

Take time now to estimate your day's tasks. I'll get a cup of coffee while you do that.

Key Takeaways From Step 2

- For every single task, write down a time estimate of no less than 5 minutes and no more than 2 hours.
- Be crystal clear about what "done" means for each task.
- Keep tasks small. That will keep your schedule flexible, and every task you complete will add to your motivation.
- Only estimate the work you do yourself, not what you delegate to others.

Step 3: Order Your Work

The eight-hour day is a myth

Here's What You Do:

- Plan for no more than 6 hours of productive work. The 8-hour day is a myth.
- Include every single demand on your time.
- Take a blank sheet of paper. This will represent today. Put your 2 most important sticky-note tasks at the top left.
- Always display today's sheet in plain sight.
- Create a separate sheet for each of the other days of the week.
- Plan your entire week as best you know it today, then let it evolve.

The Story

In 2006 I was working as a project manager for a large pharmaceutical company. I managed multiple projects for multiple teams, and coordinated my activities with Mike, another project manager in the same area. He and I had spent time at Menlo Innovations, a small software development company in Ann Arbor, Michigan. It was there that we learned and implemented their Agile approach to software development.

Everything Menlo does to manage projects is thoroughly physical and actively hands-on. In particular, Mike and I were impressed with a method they used called the Planning Game. With it they would do a weekly review and then order their project work, all using large 11x17 planning sheets.

The sheets represented budgeted resources. The work itself was represented with story cards, which were filled out and arranged onto the large sheets. Everything was broken down by what could be accomplished within one to two weeks. The whole process was fully and completely tactile.

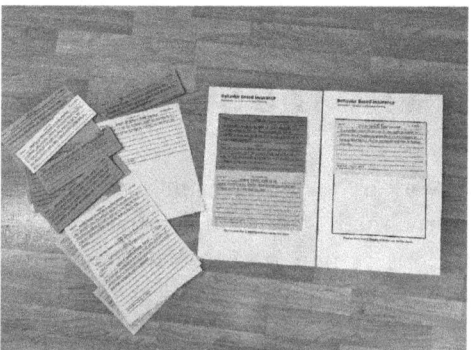

We adopted this and began using it for our weekly planning. We wrote our tasks on to sheets of paper. We sized our tasks in increments of hours; one hour, four hours, eight hours. We folded our sheets of paper to represent the sizing. Our 11x17 planning sheets represented one week of our time. We placed our tasks onto the planning sheets at the beginning of every week. We quickly learned that not everything would fit into our respective weekly plannings sheets. This resulted in decisions about what needed to get done.

Every time we did this planning, we had a far easier time making hard decisions about what work would fit into that week's plan and what would have to be addressed the following week. Anyone who has worked as a project manager knows that *this is the holy grail of planning*, enabling your team to make firm and confident decisions.

Not surprisingly, Mike and I started planning all our individual and collective tasks this way, using planning sheets and posting them on the wall above our desks. It was an incredibly effective system of managing our own daily work. Working on similar projects we now had a way to avoid duplication of work or, worse, missing something critical. We backed each other up on projects, providing an alternate project manager if either of us was out for the day. Best of all, we were able to complete every day's work without ever spending extra hours at the office.

When I started doing more work from home and became overwhelmed with my own daily responsibilities, I put the same method to work yet again, and took back control of my time.

The The Art of Agile Living method you're learning is a hybrid of kanban and Menlo's brilliant Planning Game. In this and later chapters you'll see how we apply these various concepts.

So What About All These Sticky Notes?

At this point you should have a nice collection of sticky notes with time estimates. Thankfully, I have a simple method to organize them. I call it my **7-Sheet Plan**.

Gather seven sheets of 8.5x11 or A4 unlined paper. Printer paper works well for this.

Let's imagine today is Monday. Take the first sheet and label it "Monday" at the top.

Your sticky notes for today's tasks will go here, in the order you plan to do them. (More on that in a moment.)

You have six sheets left. Label those with the other weekdays: Tuesday, Wednesday, Thursday, Friday. Then with the remaining two sheets, label one Weekend and the other Backlog.

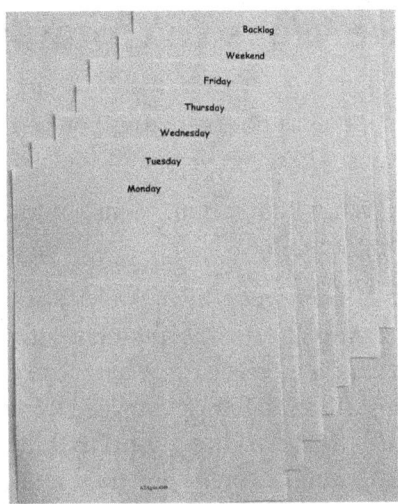

This gives you a visual weekly schedule for your work.

Many of us love to use technological tools for managing our to-do items. So we keep our tasks digital—stored neatly on a laptop, a phone, or a tablet.

But there's a problem with that: Any list of items you put on a computer or device disappears instantly from sight with the click of a button or the closing of a screen. And as we know, out of sight is *out of mind*.

And when something is out of mind, it doesn't get done. That's why I display my 7-Sheet Plan in plain sight, on my desk, throughout the week. And the sheets are reusable.

On Monday I have the Monday sheet there on top. The activities I've scheduled for that day are there in plain sight, all day, sitting on my desk, no matter what is displayed on my computer or phone. That lets me focus on today and today only.

And the way that my "today" is organized and presented to me becomes a critical factor on my ability to focus and get work done.

Two Ways to Organize

There are two approaches to organizing your daily work: **prioritizing** and **ordering**. These are very different.

Prioritizing asks, "What is *important* to me?" Ordering asks, "What *sequence* am I going to follow?"

Answering the call from your boss is likely more "important"—or certainly more pressing in the moment—than checking your email inbox. But this can be tricky. What's truly "important" also depends on the time frame. There are always things that need to get done today that may not be as "important" as things you'll complete next week, next year, or beyond. But they still have to get done today.

To illustrate, I recently wrote out this task "Evaluate my investment funds and identify two areas for improvement so that I have enough money to retire."

> *Evaluate my investment funds and identify 2 areas for improvement so that I have enough money to retire.*

This is supremely important; nobody will argue that. But is it more important or less important than "Attend the client meeting today"?

I can think of a lot of tasks where this becomes a difficult question. I quickly realize that a task's importance is not the only factor in organizing my work.

This is where I use **ordering** to help me manage my day. I'll order my tasks based on a few key questions:

- Which tasks are *important,* and which tasks are just "nice to have"?
- When during the day does each task need to be done?
- How quick or easy will a task be to complete?

The first items I put on the sheet are time-based events, such as attending the client meeting at 1:00 p.m. Depending on when during the day these are scheduled, they may go higher or lower on my sheet.

Once those are in place I put down my *important* tasks somewhere on the page (not necessarily at the top). Everything else gets arranged around these.

For tasks that take only a few minutes to complete, I'll likely put them in the remaining gaps and open spaces. I might even block off a thirty- or sixty-minute slot every day for all the "quick stuff."

As for the task where I evaluate my investment funds, I consider that *important* but flexible. I schedule it around my day's work where it makes the most sense. This could be on my lunch break or during early evening. I can even move it to the weekend. The key is that I've designated a time for it, and it will get done this week.

Launching the Perfect Monday

Let's imagine we're just kicking off the week. Take a look at your sticky note collection of tasks with their estimates. Based on ordering and relative prioritization, grab your Monday sheet and place the two items you most clearly need to do today at the very top of it.

Now look at the rest of your sticky notes. Do a quick mental ordering: What else needs to get done *today?* What is a reasonable order in which to do those tasks? Place those items on the Monday page in a column, one after the other, starting down the left side.

Step 3: Order Your Work

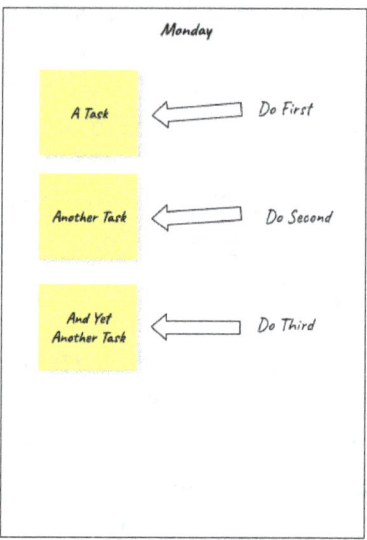

If you run out of room on the page, that's a sign that you've probably scheduled too much for the day. So move the rest of your sticky notes onto the pages for the remainder of the week.

When you originally defined your work for this week, you may have created twenty, thirty, fifty or more sticky notes. Don't be surprised if your Monday sheet contains just eight of those.

Don't Miss Your Big Scheduled Items

I created two new sticky notes when making my Monday page; "Gather materials for first meeting," estimated at five minutes, and "Attend first meeting," estimated at one hour. The meeting was already in my calendar but I put it on my planning sheet because I wanted to make it visible as part of my day.

This is a *very important* aspect to our planning that we often neglect. We grab from a list of items to do and then schedule more than we can finish in a day because *we simply forget the other demands on our time.*

Every meeting you attend should be on your page. Every demand on your time should be reflected on your sheet.

Having said that, you're likely reading this because you're doing work at home. So what about natural daily habits, such as taking a shower, getting dressed, getting to school or work, or exercising? You'll notice these items aren't on my sheet. Should they be on yours?

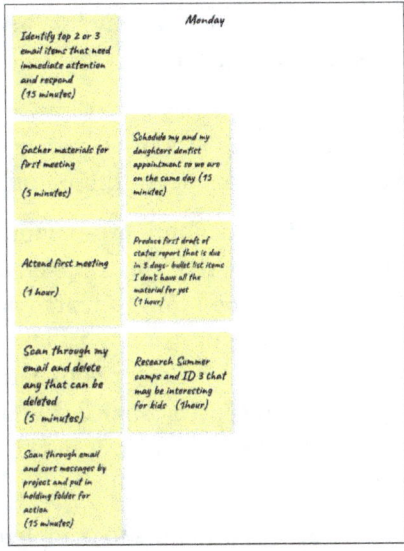

They might be. It all depends on where you are on your journey of managing chaos!

I suggest starting with the bigger tasks that are *not* natural daily habits. If exercising is not already part of your familiar routine but you want it to be, write a task for it and include it on your daily schedule. Most people shower and eat every day already, so you may be fine leaving those off your sheet.

However, if I've scheduled a special lunch with a colleague, I will include it on my schedule to reflect that it's a unique demand on my time.

The Myth of the 8-Hour Day

How much time do you really have in a day to complete your work? You might assume that if you work full time, eight hours of your day is allocated for your job. That might leave another two to four hours outside of that for personal get-it-done activities.

But does reality actually work that way? When I plan based on these assumptions, I often find myself overscheduling my time. What's going on here?

The fact is that out of eight hours of allocated work time, you're likely productive for only about six of those hours, if that.

You may be unaware of the volume of unplanned activities your workday is actually filled with: checking email and acting on it, answering the phone, responding to texts and chats and Slack messages, plus all those pop-in visits by colleagues. This doesn't cover trips to the washroom, breaks for coffee, time to just sit and think through issues, or the occasional lap you take around the office to stretch your legs and clear your mind because you've been sitting for so long.

If you attempt to schedule eight hours to complete your work tasks and then another two to four hours for your personal activities—for a total of ten to twelve hours in a day—you will end up overscheduled.

Start With Six

Aim smaller. Set a hard limit for your first week of this process: plan on no more than six hours of job-related work and two or three hours of home or leisure activities afterward.

Then observe. Gather some data. Adjust the maximum number of hours you schedule in a day, based on what actually happens in *your* real world.

Once you've established that, plan every day of your week the same way. Yours might start to look like the example below. Note that not every day will be full, at least not on Monday. Don't worry—as the week progresses you'll discover more tasks and add more items to your 7-Sheet Plan.

Remember, the goal here is to *not* overschedule ourselves. We want to manage our overwhelm and get more done by being intentional and focused. This process gives us time to do the truly important things such as exercising, being with our families, and enjoying our lives.

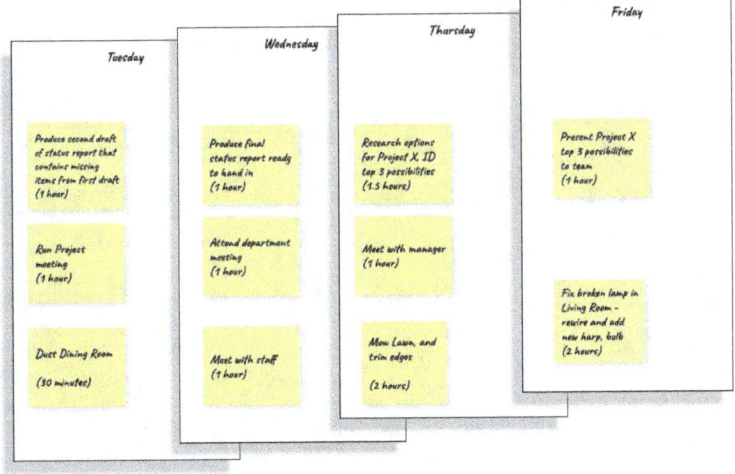

Key Takeaways From Step 3

- The 8-hour day is a myth. Plan for no more than 6 hours of productive work.
- Start with a small number of items on your daily plan, and increase them as you learn what you can get done.
- Put your 2 most important items at the top of today's page.
- Include every single demand on your time.
- Always display today's sheet in plain sight.
- Plan your entire week as best you know it today, then let it evolve.

Sidebar: Out of Sight, Out of Mind By Bryan Todd

Building focus by removing distractions

Previously we warned you against something we call "out of sight, out of mind." What we mean is this: When you think of a task that needs to be done, or you have a new project idea, write it down immediately. Put it someplace where you'll see it and act on it. Otherwise it'll be lost and forgotten—out of sight, out of mind—and will never get done.

There's another meaning to "out of sight, out of mind," but it's a positive one. I learned this from David Allen and his book *Getting Things Done*. And it's perfectly consistent with The Art of Agile Living.

He *wants* you to get stuff "out of sight, out of mind." But what he means is, write it down. Plan it, schedule it, so you can forget about it until the appropriate time that you'll be reminded to take action on it. That way it doesn't buzz around in your head, it doesn't bother you, and it doesn't distract you.

Again, this is totally consistent with The Art of Agile Living. When you've done the process right, in your off hours you won't be thinking about unfinished stuff. And during your working hours you'll only be thinking about the present task at hand.

This was reinforced for me recently when I decided to adopt Helene's method, her 7-sheet plan. It helped cement it permanently in my thinking.

You see, when I first started doing kanban, I used a familiar old board method that I saw online. I took a pad of paper, turned it to landscape orientation, and divided it up into columns: Backlog, Today, Doing, Blocked, Done.

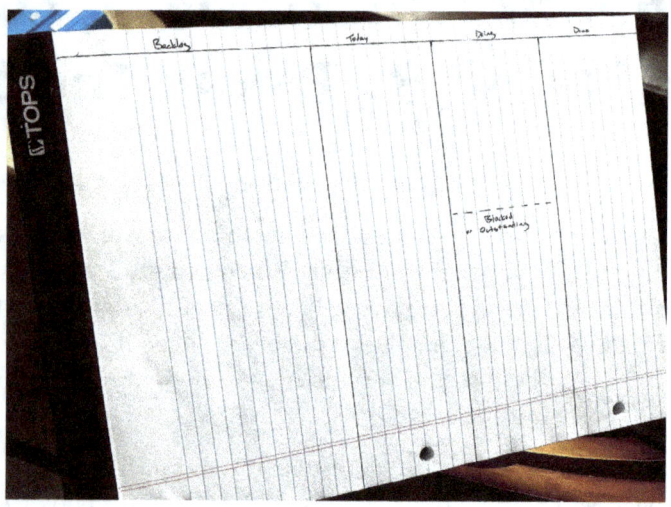

Kanban was totally new to me, and I liked the method. A lot. It allowed me to always focus on one key task at a time.

But I quickly ran into problems. There wasn't enough room for all my sticky notes under any one day, even if I used tiny little Post-It™ page markers.

Also, it didn't give me separate days of the week to plan for. That meant that every undone item just got stuck under Backlog.

And guess what? My backlog filled up almost overnight. And if I got an idea for something new that needed to be done, there wasn't room for it. My backlog was backlogged!

That's no good. So I decided that it was time to follow the The Art of Agile Living method in full, as Helene and Tom teach.

With that approach, you don't use one sheet, you use seven. That's five separate full-size sheets for each weekday, plus a weekend sheet, and then your backlog sheet.

This turned out to be the solution. I could take my big pile of backlog sticky notes and start spacing my tasks out throughout the week. There was plenty of room on each day's sheet of paper for everything necessary.

I watched as my number of backlog items shrank down to a small handful. Now I no longer had to worry about overloading it with task ideas. I could have as many new ideas as I wanted.

But there's one other detail that made this extra valuable: I schedule my tasks and then *store all my sheets inside my folder.* Everything except today's sheet. That sits on top of the folder, on my desk in plain view.

Now today's tasks are the only thing I see.

Future tasks are certainly there in the folder if I want to check on them. But there's no backlog piling up in front of me. I don't see tomorrow's work or any other stuff from the rest of the week. It's taken care of. Gone from view.

And on today's sheet, as I finish my tasks, I move each item over from the left to the right. I get to the end of my day and the left side of my sheet is clean and empty. Nothing else I have to do. Nothing else I have to think about.

Everything else that I'll be working on in the coming days is—for now—out of sight, out of mind.

That is stress-free work.

Sidebar: The Eisenhower Principle

Ordering Important versus Urgent tasks

In 1945 Dwight D. Eisenhower[1] referred to Dr J. Roscoe Miller, president of Northwestern University, in stating that "I have two kinds of problems: the urgent and the important. The urgent are not important, and the important are never urgent." His approach using only these two criteria, urgency and importance, has become known as the Eisenhower Principle[2].

Utilizing this method, you can order your work based on its relative importance versus urgency:

- Work that is Important and Urgent gets ordered first
- Work that is Important but not Urgent, gets ordered second
- Work that is Urgent by not Important, gets ordered third
- And work that is neither Important nor Urgent gets ordered fourth

---

[1] Dwight D. Eisenhower, the supreme commander of the World War II Allied Expeditionary Force, and 34th president of the United States.

[2] https://www.mindtools.com/al1e0k5/eisenhowers-urgentimportant-principle

Sidebar: The Eisenhower Principle

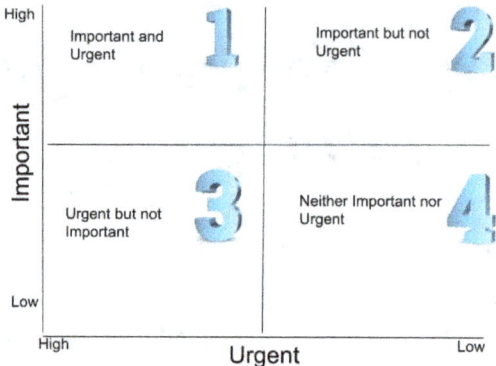

Using this chart helps to quickly order your work based on only two factors, importance and urgency. For example, calling a plumber to fix a broken water pipe is an urgent and important task, this would go into the first quadrant.

The task to "evaluate my investments funds so that I have enough money to retire" is important but not urgent. It would go into the second quadrant. A request to complete a task today from a co-worker may be urgent but not necessarily important. This one goes into the third quadrant, (particularly as I gently suggest delegating it to someone else). The fourth quadrant is used for those tasks that are neither urgent nor important. These generally are the nice to haves on your to-do list.

The first items to put on the sheet are urgent and time-based events, such as attending the client meeting at 1:00 p.m. Depending on when during the day these are scheduled, they may go higher or lower on your sheet.

Once those are in place, evaluate and put down your *important but not urgent* tasks and determine where it makes the most sense to schedule these, and place them somewhere on the page (not necessarily at the top). Then come my *urgent but not important* tasks. Everything else gets arranged around these.

> *Evaluate my investment funds and identify 2 areas for improvement so that I have enough money to retire.*

This method provides a quick way to order your tasks. It is not a pedantic approach, however. All quadrant 2 items are not necessarily on the sheet for today. For example, the task to *evaluate my investments*, while important and in quadrant 2, the time to complete it is flexible. It may get scheduled for today during lunch or after dinner, or may even move to the weekend.

The key is that you have evaluated every task and have allocated time to complete them.

Step 4: Do Your Work

Focus on one task at a time

Here's What You Do:

- Do one task at a time, working on each one until it's complete.
- Mark each finished sticky-note item as done and physically move it to the right side of the sheet.
- When surprises and unplanned events come up, write them down, estimate their time, and put them in order.
- Postpone or delegate any item you're unable to complete within your scheduled workday.

The Story

Starting in early 2020 my mask making process became a hobby, a relaxing nightly routine. After dinner each evening I would head up to my sewing room and get to work.

Once I had been doing this for several months, I started to get a little cocky with my abilities. I brought in my iPad and streamed shows to watch while I sewed. I figured mask making was almost muscle memory. What could go wrong?

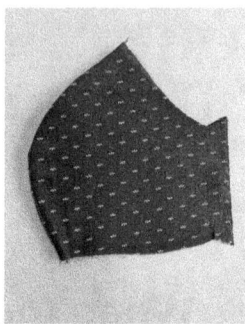

Figure 1. The outside of the mask

I always make each mask from two kinds of cloth, a liner and the outer fabric. One evening as I sat preparing the liner for a mask, I was especially distracted by "The Great British Baking Show." My mind wandered from my work and I fixated on the breads the contestants were preparing on screen, watching them measure, mix, knead, proof, and bake. I was entranced.

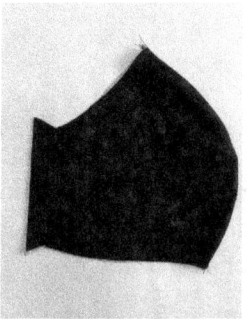

Figure 2. The intended liner of the mask

Then I looked down. What I had intended to make was a mask with liner on the inside and decorative cloth on the outside. What I had actually stitched together was a full mask with liner on the left, main cloth on the right.

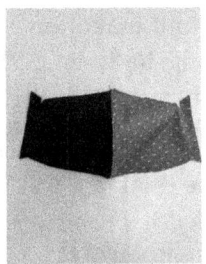

Figure 3. The resultant mask

Totally wrong. I had just created waste. All because I was distracted by the show.

Specifically I had asked my brain to **multitask**, to focus on two things at the same time.

I know from years of Agile experience that this is never a good idea, yet even I could not resist the temptation. As a result I had proved yet again that our brains really do only handle one complex task at a time.

In attempting to multitask, I ended up with a face mask that serves only as an illustration for this book.

This philosophy of focusing on one thing at a time acknowledges a genuine human constraint. We need to focus. Focus is at the heart of all Agile thinking. And Agile encourages us to apply it to all of our daily work.

One Thing, and One Thing Only

Grab your task sheet for today. Once you have your day mapped out, *start with the single item at the top of your list.* Do not stop until you complete it.

Do one thing at a time. There are a number of benefits to this:

You free up your brain and make fewer mistakes. Studies show that continually switching between tasks increases the time to complete each task and increases cognitive impairment[1].

The human brain cannot multitask efficiently. It handles one thing at a time. Try to do more than one task at a time and you'll only split your focus. When that happens, you lose motivation and you make mistakes.

When you work on a single task, you're 100% effective. With no other demands on your time, you can give it your full energy and attention.

Tasks get completed sooner. If you switch back and forth between two tasks, you'll find yourself losing time. How is this?

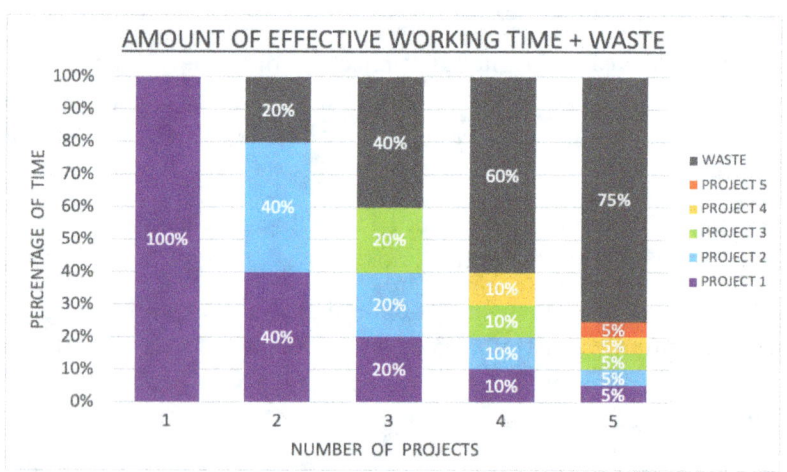

An effective visual of the impact of constantly switching between work projects. The chart is from Matt Lasater of Engaged Agility, adapted from the book Quality Software Management: Systems Thinking *by Gerald Weinberg.*

Imagine that you work partway through task one. Then you drop it and pick up task two. You finish it and go back to task one, but

---

[1] *https://www.nytimes.com/2008/10/25/business/yourmoney/25shortcuts.html* and http://news.stanford.edu/2009/08/24/multitask-research-study-082409/

your progress was interrupted. You now have to reorient yourself and get back up to speed on the original task. You've lost valuable minutes and precious mental energy.

Let's call that "switching time." Multiply the number of tasks you're working on at any one time, and you'll find that your switching time will exceed the time you would have spent completing any one task.

Once you're spinning four or more separate plates at once, you've increased your switching time to 60% and succeeded in making yourself feel the least motivated, least effective, least focused, and least satisfied with your progress.

Very simply, focus on one thing at a time and *work gets done faster.* This is the key concept of Agile, Lean, and kanban systems thinking.

You experience more items marked as "done." If you agree to give yourself these two core constraints,

1. Only work on one task at a time
2. No single task can take you more than two hours

that will force you to take larger complex tasks and break them down into pieces that fit both constraints. Suddenly, large intimidating blobs of work become manageable, doable items that you know you can finish inside of two hours.

And now every two hours, *check!* another item is marked complete. This is a wonderful discipline that will reinforce for you that *you are getting things done.*

I learned my lesson about getting too absorbed in a TV show when I'm doing sewing projects. I sometimes still have entertainment playing in the background while I work; I like the social noise. But now I make it something light enough that I can largely ignore it.

Step 4: Do Your Work

Physically Mark It and Move It

As you complete each item on your daily sheet, put a check mark on it, move it to the right side of the paper, and start working on the next item on your list.

This is kinesthetics at its best. Moving the physical task to "done" on the right side of the planning sheet makes the abstract real. It gives your brain a mental kick. You get a new dose of motivation to pick up and work on the next task. The fact that you are making physical progress is clear and unmistakable.

Repeat this process until either:

- all the items on your list are completed, or
- you've reached the end of the day.

If you've finished more than you had planned and you still have time left in your day, feel free to pull something off tomorrow's sheet and work on it now. You're getting ahead!

Expect Surprises, and Add Them to Your List

Like you, I always think I know what my day is going to look like. And then surprises or unplanned events pop up. When these happen, I just follow my process: Write down each new item, estimate it, and order the work.

For each new task I ask myself, Does this need to be done today? If the answer is yes, I decide what other tasks I'll *remove* from today's schedule in order to make room for the new one.

Remember: the goal is to *not* overschedule ourselves. If the task does not need to be done today, I'll move it to one of the other days on my weekly schedule, further adjusting my weekly plan to accommodate the change.

Get Your Life Back: Delegate!

We're giving you back ownership of your life. When a surprise task comes up, it's not okay to just say, "I'll work through dinner" or, "I'll skip my daughter's track meet."

No. You now have too much work for today. Move it to another day and enjoy your evening.

> *Schedule sons dental cleaning appointment*
>
> *Give to husband*

Even better, these can be opportunities to enlist the help of others. I shared with you the example of scheduling my son's dental appointment. I delegated that to my husband.

That's just one of many such opportunities. Look for these in your daily life. You may be surprised at how much those around you are willing to help. It's a great feeling when you sense that your family is eager to pitch in to get work done.

Key Takeaways From Step 4

- Do one task at a time. This lets you complete each item faster, with fewer mistakes.
- Mark each completed item as done and physically move it. This feeds your motivation.
- When surprises and unplanned events pop up, write them down, estimate their time, and order them.
- Postpone or delegate any item you're unable to complete within your scheduled workday.

Sidebar: A Princess and a Hippopotamus

The art of letting go

The Scrum Princess by Kyle and Demi Aretae is written as a child's book that introduces simple project management principles. It follows a young princess who has a kingdom and lots of gold.

She sees a host of things she would like improved. So she calls in her wizard and tells him everything she wants: her rickety carriage fixed, a new well dug, the castle roof repaired, a fence around her cattle, and a pet hippopotamus to frolic in the pasture.

A royal Scrum team is assembled to look into her requests. They share their findings with her.

"Fixing the carriage is easiest," they tell her. "We can do that fast.

But the hippopotamus will take almost forever. Africa is far away."

The Princess protests. She very much wants a hippo.

Her wizard reminds her, "Princess, you may specify in what order your wishes are fulfilled, but you may not change how far away Africa is."

The story is a lesson in choosing priorities and focusing on the best tasks. It teaches a very simple reality we face when we have long lists of things we'd like done: We may have people around us willing to help, and lots of resources available, but each of us can only do one thing at a time. So how do we choose what's most important?

After some back and forth, the princess accepts her royal team's recommendations and they get to work. To her delight, the carriage, the castle roof, and the fence are completed in due time. And in place of a well, her people build a much cheaper new canal.

Amid the busyness, the Princess forgets all about the hippo. Some time later she's reminded of it.

"Oh that silly idea," she says. "Let's throw that away."

The metaphor of the hippo is a valuable one. It represents so many things we want where it becomes clear that the thing is nice to have but not essential. Or, in some cases, there may have been a strong need for it at one time but the need no longer exists.

Making wish lists is a good thing. But always keep your eye out for hippos. Be flexible and willing to let go of things that might be nice to have but ultimately aren't worth the fuss.

Get the full story at *https://thescrumprincess.com*[1]

---

[1] https://thescrumprincess.com

Step 5: Review Your Day

Daily reflection and feedback

Here's What You Do:

- Take time at the end of each day for reflection and feedback.
- Start by asking if your most important tasks got done.
- Evaluate how accurate your time estimates were.
- Learn what your most frequent barriers to completion are.
- Find the best times of day for doing your most important tasks.
- Identify where you need extra time for breaks and rest, and for unexpected events.

The Principle

The end of my day is a special time. That's when I review the tasks that didn't get done. You read me right: I often have tasks that *did not* get accomplished.

This may be true for you too, especially if you're new to this process. You're still discovering your personal cadence; you may get to the end of your day and find that you haven't completed everything you had planned.

In my case, I recognize that there's a variety of reasons why my tasks may not get accomplished during the day. Rather than beating myself up for not finishing everything as I had planned,

I use the time for reflection. I spend a few minutes asking myself these questions:

- Did my most important tasks get done?
- Which tasks were the easiest to complete?
- Which tasks did I enjoy the most?
- Which tasks did I enjoy the least?
- How was my motivation with each of today's tasks?
- What may have contributed to my not completing all the tasks on my daily sheet?

These are great questions for reflection. They let me acknowledge everything I *did* get done, and how much I did or did not enjoy the process.

The very last question is what the rest of this chapter is about.

Break the Barriers to Completion

I take a positive approach. I focus on teasing out and eliminating things that have prevented me from getting my work done. I call these my "barriers to completion": anything and everything today that blocked me, distracted me, drained my motivation, interrupted me, or otherwise got in the way.

At the end of my workday I go through my tasks and identify barriers to completion. If I take the right action today, they won't be a problem tomorrow.

Using the following principles, I can spot where I got blocked or stuck.

Pick the right time of day for your most important tasks. There's a reason why the first question on the list above is "Did my most important tasks get done today?" The key is to place the most mission-critical tasks on your daily planning sheet where you're in the best frame of mind to complete them.

If you are a morning person, like me, you may want to put the day's most critical items at the top of your planning sheet, and tackle them early. If you shine in the afternoons, save your gotta-do's for when you have the most energy and motivation to accomplish them.

Know your motivators. Motivation is a complex subject. Let me start by introducing you to a simple either-or: Are you extrinsically or intrinsically motivated?

The other day I baked a fresh loaf of bread for my neighbor. Seeing the delight on their face when I brought it over was a wonderful motivator for me. I went back home and mixed, prepared, and baked yet another loaf for my son and daughter-in-law.

That's a form of extrinsic motivation. It comes from outside yourself. It's about pleasing others, and seeing how others respond to things you do.

Intrinsic motivation is when pleasing yourself is enough to keep you going. If the simple act of ticking items off a checklist gets you motivated and happy, then this is you.

Extrinsic motivation is about finding joy from pleasing others. If you do best when others are depending on you, then you're more driven by extrinsic motivators.

Intrinsic motivation is about elevating your own standards and meeting your own goals.

Your workday will have both: items where you're called on to meet others' requirements, and items where it's about fulfilling your own. Some you'll like more; others you'll like less. Know which is which, and you can sequence your work and break up the rhythm of your day by interspersing enjoyable tasks with the ones that are less so.

Gretchin Rubin's wonderful book *The Four Tendencies: The Indispensable Personality Profiles That Reveal How to Make Your Life Better (and Other People's Lives Better, Too)* describes the intrinsic and extrinsic motivators that drive our behavior. This is recommended reading if you continually find yourself with tasks left unfinished at the end of the day and all you know is that you just didn't "feel" like doing them.

Each of us are driven by different motivators in different situations. Explore and learn where and how each one drives you, and you'll eliminate more barriers to completion.

Estimate your time accurately. Sometimes you simply underestimate the amount of time it will take to finish a task. That can be frustrating, but if you're clear on how it happened, that's good information.

When I do my end-of-day review, I go over the estimates I had put down for today's work. I compare them to how long each task actually took me. Then I set tomorrow's estimates accordingly.

Keep tasks small. When you ask yourself, "Which tasks were the easiest to complete?" I'm willing to bet that your answer is almost always "The smallest ones." The ease of a task almost always correlates with its size. Smaller, shorter tasks are easier to finish.

We're far more motivated to start into a ten-minute task than one we know will take thirty minutes. That alone is reason enough to break your work into smaller pieces wherever you can.

Toss out the "hippos." You'll be surprised how much you find that your planning sheets include hippos[1]. These are tasks that we initially capture and track, but over time realize that they don't actually need to get done.

Take a moment and ask yourself if you've created any hippos for your work. Are there tasks on your sheet where circumstances

---

[1]From the book *The Scrum Princess* by Kyle and Demi Aretae, https://thescrumprincess.com.

have changed and you no longer need them? Be courageous. Give yourself permission to throw out tasks that you no longer want or need done.

Delegate. It's a safe bet you have unfinished tasks where you can ask, "Could someone else handle this task instead of me?" and the answer is yes. Perhaps your spouse or partner can take your son to his dentist appointment, for example.

If your children are old enough, they may enjoy being given a task like, say, researching the best summer camps. (Be sure you define their boundaries, though. They may decide that the best "summer camp" is to book three months on the islands of Fiji!)

Give yourself space. Very broadly speaking, I may look back over the day and find that I just wasn't particularly motivated. I did everything else right—I planned my most important tasks for the right time of day; I was keenly aware of my motivators; I estimated accurately; I kept my tasks small; I eliminated hippos; I delegated what I could. And still, a lot of my work felt like a drag.

When this happens, I'll take a few extra moments to explore why. Perhaps I need to schedule more free time in my day. Maybe some exercise, fresh air, and sunshine will pick up my mood. It could be that today's rainy weather slowed me down.

Knowing that tomorrow will be a brighter day, I give myself some slack and rearrange my schedule for the rest of the week to allow more breaks and variety.

Recognize when "life happens." Sometimes completely unexpected things come up. A family member might need your immediate help, and that takes precedence over your planned activities. I fully realize that life still happens, despite all our best planning efforts.

But note: If you are always pushing tasks off to the next day, something is broken. This is the time and place to fix it. If you constantly leave yourself in this state, you're simply building bad habits.

Gretchin Rubin's *The Four Tendencies* may be just the right resource for you on breaking out of habits like these. Also, in an upcoming chapter we talk about the buddy system and personal accountability. That can be a key that helps you stick with the process and enjoy its many benefits.

Make an effort to complete every task on your sheet at least every other day. This is the The Art of Agile Living process done right. It will feed your internal and external motivators, and you'll feel more eagerness to get tasks done in the future.

How to Finish Out Your Day

Rearrange the items on your upcoming day sheets, and move things to your backlog as needed. Take hippos off your list and throw them away.

You don't have to keep working through the night to complete everything on your sheet. You don't have to continually keep moving tasks to the next day, never seeing them completed. The Art of Agile Living serves you, not the other way around. Follow these principles and you'll find that you can plan your day, finish your work within your scheduled time, and go about your life without stress and overwhelm.

Key Takeaways From Step 5

- Take time at the end of each day for reflection and feedback.
- Start by asking if your most important tasks got done.
- Learn what your most frequent barriers to completion are.
- Identify where you're intrinsically or extrinsically motivated.
- Leave room for breaks and rest, and for unexpected events.

Step 6: Update Your Backlog

A place for near-term and longer-term items

Here's What You Do:

- Create a "backlog" sheet for necessary items that don't have to be done this week.
- Include both near-term and longer-term items, no matter how large.
- Break items down, then estimate them and put them in sequence.
- Update your backlog at the beginning of every week, moving tasks onto your daily plan sheets.
- Create a separate backlog sheet if you have a major project.

The Story

I've always liked to think of myself as a superb organizer. With every day of the week planned out, I've always been good at getting my tasks done for the week.

But I had a good reminder recently. A jolt of reality, actually. My car tire blew out, leaving me stranded on the roadside. I suddenly remembered that I had intended weeks earlier to go looking for new tires.

Step 6: Update Your Backlog

A similar thing happened last summer. There was a resort we had wanted to go to for our vacation, but when I went online to make reservations I discovered they were booked solid. I had intended to take care of this two months earlier, but forgot.

Sometimes I forget to make use of all the tools I have available to me from the Agile toolkit. It happens to the best of us. For starters, this was a great reminder to me to always keep sticky notes handy, to always have a way to write down a new task when the thought occurs to me.

Do you need to research an important purchase? Put it on a sticky note. Do you need a reminder to book something in advance? Write it down immediately.

And then life can get complicated. Maybe you've written down a task, but your schedule is packed full and you know you won't get the item done this week.

If that's the case, you've now uncovered a very common timescale planning issue. And there's a solution: a place to store this and other tasks like it.

Not everything we need to do in life can be finished inside a single week. With that in mind, the Agile toolkit has given us a place to write down and park tasks that involve a bigger time frame—a longer "planning horizon."

Enter the Backlog Planning Sheet

You'll recall that in Step 3 I invited you to create seven daily planning sheets, one of them called "Backlog." Here's where this becomes invaluable.

The backlog sheet is for items that need to get done but don't have to happen *this week*. It's your list of *upcoming* items and events.

Anything and everything you can think of that will need to be done in the next several weeks, or even months—here's where you get it out of your head and onto paper. Every item that occurs to you, especially the big ones.

From there you break tasks down and then estimate and order them. That way they don't get lost or forgotten. I do this with my daily planning sheets, and I do it on my backlog sheet as well.

If an item is too large to estimate, I still put it on the backlog. You know: the "buy a new car," "paint the house," and "plan next year's family vacation" types of items.

Again: for any project or task that you intend to have done

sometime in the future but don't want to forget, write it on a sticky note and add it to your backlog.

Break it Into Pieces

Some of these will be longer-term items. If "paint the house" is a project I'm looking to schedule within the next couple of months, I can start to break it down now into actionable items, the same way I always do for the current week's tasks. Paint the house becomes: "Visit paint store and get tester samples of 3 candidate colors (1 hour); Paint small sections of house with each of the candidate colors (2 hours); Get 2-3 quotes from candidate painters (30 minutes); Schedule Painter (20 minutes)".

| Visit paint store and get tester samples of 3 candidate colors (1 hour) | Paint small sections of house with each of the candidate colors (2 hours) | get 2-3 quotes from candidate painters (30 minutes) | schedule painter (20 minutes) |

My near-term items get estimates as well. Because these are smaller and more immediately actionable, I can fit them into my standard limits of between five minutes and two hours.

The larger items just sit there as reminders of projects that need to be evaluated, scheduled, or discarded.

This is Actually Ideal

My backlog is now looking like a mix of near-term actionable items and larger long-term goals. That's not only okay; it's ideal.

I know far more about items happening in the next five to ten days than those scheduled out weeks into the future. I focus on the near-term items; they're less likely to change. It's worth my time to break these down and have them ready for an upcoming week.

It's my larger, future items that are more likely either to change or to be removed from my list entirely. And that's where I need to be cautious: time spent detailing something that could undergo major changes, or be discarded completely, is time wasted. Like you, I'm all about spending my time wisely.

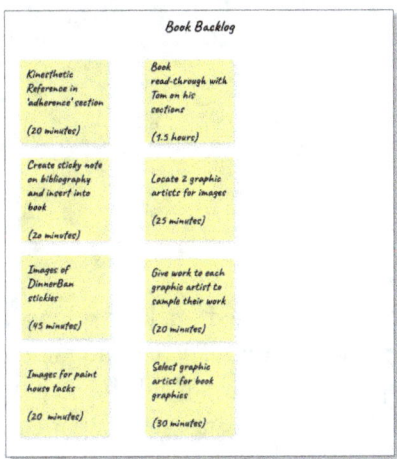

And Not Just One Sheet!

After I had been following this process for a couple of years, I noticed that my backlog was starting to grow beyond one sheet of paper. With all of my plans and ideas for house projects and work projects, I saw that some of them were not getting the attention they deserved.

That's when I started using separate backlog sheets for separate major projects.

In fact, I created a backlog sheet for writing this book. At the top of it I wrote, "Book Backlog." On it were all the individual tasks related to the book—stories to insert, pictures to create, proofreading times, text to adjust, and more.

New Condo Backlog

Select new kitchen appliances - visit 2 stores and select one (2 hours)	Fix stucco on lanai - over door (1.5 hours)	Test sample color on wall in new condo (30 minutes)
Get new hot water heater installed (1 hour)	Fix stucco on lanai over window (2 hours)	Get quotes from 2 painters for new condo (30 minutes)
Purchase new cabinet handles (1 hour)	Get quote from movers (25 minutes)	Schedule painter (10 minutes)
Install new cabinet handles (1.5 hours)	Schedule movers (15 minutes)	Move day (6 hours)

Likewise, when we started making plans to purchase another condominium, the amount of scheduling and coordination became overwhelming. So I wrote out all the steps related to selling our current condo and purchasing the new one, and I placed them on a separate backlog sheet titled "New Condo Backlog." Things like 'Select new kitchen appliances; Get new hot water heater installed; and Purchase new cabinet handles.

That greatly enhanced my focus for that activity. During my weekly planning sessions (which I'll describe in a moment), I could now see all the steps related to each project on the separately named backlog sheets. I could decide how many to pull from each to schedule for the upcoming week. The amount of work for each project started to feel less overwhelming, and more manageable.

Longer Term Items

I was talking to my friend Gordon the other day and he shared that his backlog had indeed grown into two sheets. One for the items to be handled within the next week or two, and another for something he called his 'Deep Backlog'. Those were items that were much more longer term tasks. Things that might be a month out. Even things that were more ideas than actual tasks.

This was a similar theme with another person I chatted with recently about his backlog. He had a large list of things that he realized he might never actually do, but things he wanted to be reminded of. So he had a separate book where he wrote these down. The thought of keeping multiple records of my to-do work made me shudder a bit. The main goal of my seven sheet system is to have everything in one place. So while my friend shared this process with me, he admitted that it was not actually working so well for him. He just didn't have any better ways of handling these longer term idea-like tasks.

As I looked at my own backlog I realized that there were parts of my backlog that looked the same. I had ideas for blog posts, tasks coming up in the next couple of weeks, and monthly recurring tasks. Plus I had things that I didn't want to forget about, but were not likely to be done anytime soon. Things like 'spend 1 hour hooking up the speakers to the basement stereo system'. This is something best done during a snowy winter's day. Something I'd like to not forget about.

As I spoke with Gordon about these items that were low priority and certainly not urgent, and not likely to be scheduled in the next few weeks, we looked carefully at them and asked if we should just throw them out. Were they sparking joy in any way? Was their existence more clutter for our lives? Were they adding to our overwhelm?

While it was tempting to just toss these items, I realized that there was value in capturing these ideas. After all, they were ideas that had been in our heads. These were likely to crop up and be thought about again. These items in our heads are just the things that will distract us. They pop up when we least expect them. They take us down rabbit holes of thought, wonder, and distraction. That distraction is what stops us from keeping our focus. And losing our focus is how we stop getting our things done.

Getting things done is paramount. It's what we've been talking about throughout this entire book. So throwing these ideas and very long range tasks out doesn't seem like a very good option.

Gordon and I mused on this a bit. And as we talked, he realized that it wasn't the keeping of the items on the Deep Backlog, it was the name itself. Deep Backlog gave the impression that the items HAD to get done at some point. And that pressure, that constant reminder of these tasks and ideas, was contributing to our overwhelm. We realized the items on this deep backlog list were NOT necessarily ever going to be done. They were things we MIGHT want to do at some point. Eureka!!

I Might Want To Do Someday

Enter the 'I Might Want To Do Someday' sheet. Not things that HAVE to be done. Things I MIGHT want to do someday. Suddenly this renaming clarified our focus. This renaming gave us a more positive view of the work. Suddenly the items felt less like work related items. They felt more like play items. Something I can have fun with. Ideas I can toy around with. Ideas I can do down rabbit holes with. I've just given myself the freedom to keep these ideas and tasks, without the pressure of feeling like they ever had to be done.

The moment I got off the phone with Gordon I got out another 8x10 sheet of paper and wrote 'I Might Want To Do Someday' on the top.

I moved the longer term items and idea-like tasks off my backlog to this sheet. I took a look at my new sheet and the resultant backlog. Wow! It was incredibly liberating. I just freed my mind of these items. I freed my backlog from items. I freed my sense of **having** to accomplish all these items. I felt 20 pounds lighter.

As a result, I increased my focus on what truly needed to be accomplished. I now had more clarity on the work on my daily sheets and main backlog sheets.

All this freedom came with the recognition that some items have a need to be documented, but don't need to be done anytime soon. This liberation was the key to curbing yet more of the overwhelm impacting me on a daily basis.

Still, Beware of Multitasking

I am careful to not create too many backlog sheets, however. That would indicate that I'm slipping back into multitasking.

Recall this chart, which shows the amount of waste created when you have multiple projects running. It applies to projects you work on during a single day, and also to projects you work on over the course of several weeks, even months.

I'm careful to engage in only one or two projects at the same time. This enables me to complete them more quickly and with fewer mistakes, for reasons I explained in the chapter on Step 4.

So how many backlogs is too many? According to this chart showing the amount of effective working time and waste, if you have three projects running simultaneously then 40% of your effort is being wasted on "switching time." We recommend you use no more than two backlogs at any one time.

Step 6: Update Your Backlog

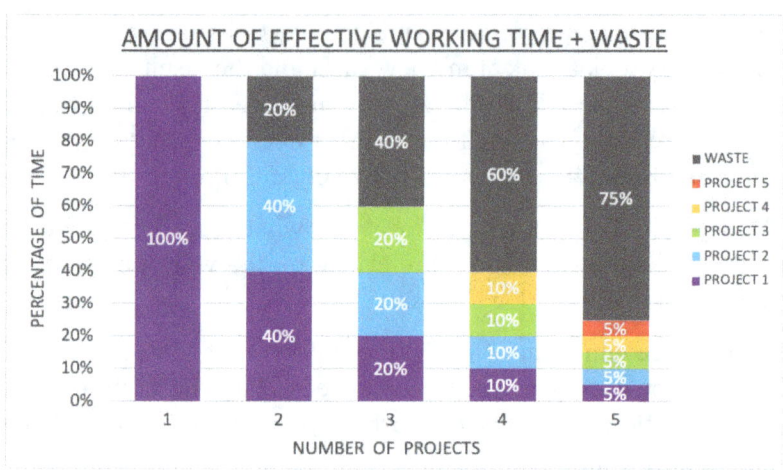

Your Weekly Planning Ceremony

At the beginning of each week I review my backlog sheets for any items that need to be added to this week's activities. This is my dedicated time to review all the items in my backlog, even the larger, longer-term ones.

It's here that I can take one of the larger items, break it down into smaller tasks, incorporate it into my week, and start working on it.

Tom and I do this as a ceremony every Monday morning. A good deal of our respective work each week involves our shared A2Agile business. By doing this together we stay accountable to each other. We're also less likely to abandon the process.

We've found this joint planning ceremony so useful that we teach it as part of our 8-week The Art of Agile Living program[1].

We also made one additional pleasant discovery recently.

---

[1] https://www.a2agile.com/agile-at-home-program

Tom observed that for his own individual tasks he can pull up his backlog on a Sunday night and plan out his Monday—and the rest of his week—right then and there.

The first time he tried this he slept extra well that night. And he showed up to his work desk Monday morning with a clear plan for the day and the week that he could launch into immediately.

Recheck Your Estimates

This is where I update my time estimates as appropriate. I may have noticed the previous week that I underestimated the time needed for a few of my tasks, and that resulted in some unfinished items.

I may also uncover a project task that upon closer inspection will take me longer than the two-hour limit. So I rewrite it, breaking it down into smaller pieces.

Reviewing my time estimates every week gives me the opportunity to adjust those estimates based on my own real working data. That in turn ensures that I can complete my tasks as planned.

Go Hippo Hunting

Time to look for hippos. Again, these are "nice to have" items that you no longer need. Find them and remove them.

Key Takeaways From Step 6

- Use your backlog sheet for necessary items that don't have to be done this week.
- Include near-term items and also longer-term items, no matter how large.

Step 6: Update Your Backlog

- Break tasks down, then estimate them and put them in sequence.
- Update your backlog sheet at the beginning of every week, incorporating those tasks into your daily plans.
- Create a separate backlog sheet if you have a major project.
- Always be hippo hunting!

Step 7: List Your Outstanding Items

Keeping track of dependencies

Here's What You Do:

- Create a larger "Outstanding Items" sticky note for tasks where you're waiting on other people.
- Write down each item, who you're waiting on, and any deadlines.
- Update the list and move it to the next sheet each day.
- Send friendly reminders where needed.

The Story

I run a local Agile Meetup group in Michigan. I often reach out to organizers of associated Meetup groups and ask them to cross-post our scheduled events. This lets us reach a broader audience.

For our last meeting I sent out one such request, asking the organizer to do us the usual favor of cross-posting. She didn't reply.

So I pinged her with a second email. Turns out she was just busy, and my initial request had fallen off her radar. She appreciated the ping, thanked me for it, and then promptly cross-posted our event.

I find this surprisingly common. Let's face it: keeping track of all our work is hard. Stuff gets forgotten. Not everyone is following the The Art of Agile Living method. So I added something special to help me track when I am waiting on others. This important little addition is what I am describing next, and I use it every single week.

When Work Involves Others

Sometimes I've finished my portion of a task and sent it to a coworker to do their part. Now I'm simply waiting for them to complete it so that I can schedule the next task.

For example, let's say that I need private network access from my place of business so that I can work from home while still accessing corporate servers and files. Accomplishing this will actually take multiple steps, some of which I can handle myself and some of which require other people.

When I break the work down, the individual tasks of "Request approval from my department head for VPN access; Request VPN access from Corporate IT; IT installs VPN on my laptop; Test VPN from off-site location" emerge . You'll notice the first three tasks require others:

[Sticky note 1: Request approval from my department head for VPN access — 15 min]
[Sticky note 2: request VPN access from Corporate IT — 5 min]
[Sticky note 3: IT installs VPN on my laptop — 30 min]
[Sticky note 4: Test VPN from off-site location — 30 min]

I can do part of the very first task—I can easily request approval from the department head. Writing and submitting the request may only take fifteen minutes. But the other person has to actually grant the approval. Waiting for that could take days.

Once I have that approval, I can immediately schedule additional tasks. But I don't want to forget that I'm waiting on it.

[Sticky note: Outstanding Items
- Dept Head, approval for VPN access]

A Special Note, Just for This

So as soon as I've submitted my "request for VPN approval" I create a new sticky note that I call "Outstanding Items." And on it I write, "Department Head: approval for VPN access."

This is an important core piece of The Art of Agile Living.

You may wonder: Why bother tracking items that are in the hands of other people? The answer is because it's something on your mind. You need to write it down so you don't lose track of it. The work is outstanding, and you need it finished before you schedule the next activity from your backlog. Staying on top of this is critical if you have hard and fast deadlines to meet.

In project management terms this is called a **dependency**. Anytime you're dependent upon something or someone, it is in your best interests to track that dependent work, so you can complete your tasks.

This is how I avoid last minute chaos. I won't let someone's lack of attention turn into my personal crisis. That's precisely what my outstanding items list does: it keeps all of a projects' dependencies on my radar.

I use a larger 3x3 sticky note for this. I write out my outstanding items—my various dependencies—and place the note visibly in the upper right on my daily sheet. I list the item, who I'm waiting on, and any deadlines associated with it.

If the person hasn't responded within the time frame I expected, and I sense this could affect my own timeline for completing a task or project, I send a reminder. I then make an additional note of that on the Outstanding Items list.

As responses come in and tasks I'm waiting on get completed, I cross them off the list. I'll rewrite the list on a new note if it begins to grow and get cluttered.

Step 7: List Your Outstanding Items

> Outstanding Items
> - Feedback from Marketing on timeline 3/31
> - Martha, when to schedule call
> - Jim, Signed quote

A typical Outstanding Items note may have a number of things listed, such as 'Feedback from Marketing on timeline 3/31; Martha, when to schedule call; and Jim, Signed quote". Each of these items are outstanding, awaiting action from someone else.

And then every day I'll *move* the Outstanding Items list to the next daily sheet. That becomes part of my daily review of the work I've completed.

By always having this visible on my daily sheet, I not only keep an eye on my own daily work but also on outstanding things that spawn new tasks. This way I can foresee delays and avoid last minute rushes.

I never allow someone else's lack of attention to be the cause of my chaos. I stay on top of them, but I do it nicely!

Key Takeaways From Step 7

- Keep track of all your dependencies with an "Outstanding Items" sticky note.
- Write down each item, who you're waiting on, and any deadlines.
- Update the list and move it to the next sheet each day.
- Send friendly reminders where needed.

Sidebar: The Corkboard Trick By Bryan Todd

A hyper-focused approach to remove distractions

There's a certain frustration I feel some days.

Let's say I've done the The Art of Agile Living process for my upcoming day. I've got my sheet, it's got my sticky notes on it, and they all have time estimates. And yet I'm still feeling some kind of internal objection, a sort of resistance. There's something about my day that's not super clear. An element missing; something fuzzy.

More often than not, in my case, it's about how much actual time the tasks will take. Yes, I've put a time estimate on each task. And yes, I can do the math, on paper or in my head.

But numbers on a piece of paper won't give me any kind of physical, visible sense of how long my tasks are going to take me. So I have a second tool. It's based on an idea I swiped from Menlo Innovations when I visited them years ago.

They do a version of this when they plan their software projects. They use pieces of paper tacked onto a large board that represent the amount of time a block of project work will take. A single piece of paper represents a day, and it can be folded up to represent a half day or quarter day.

In my case, the tool I use is my handy corkboard. I set it up years ago, and it's been sitting next to my desk for the better part of a decade now. It's faded and pocked full of pinholes, but still useful to me.

The idea is this: The three-inch width of a single 3x5 card represents an hour of my time. On my corkboard I've put up page markers, spaced the same 3 inches apart. These mark every hour of the day from 8:00 am through 1:00 pm on the left, and 2:00 pm through 7:00 pm on the right.

I take a card and write a task on it. "Email," for example. Let's say I stick it on the corkboard at the 9:30 spot. That tells me that from 9:30 to 10:30 I'll be going through my email. One hour.

If I like, I can fold the card in half to represent thirty minutes. (For this hack I never get any more granular than that.)

So imagine today is my day off. I've slept in a bit, but I have a set of tasks on paper. Also, I have a friend coming by at 1:00.

There's a whole list of things I'd like to do before he arrives, but it's all fuzzy in my head. I'm not 100% clear on what all I can actually finish in that window of time.

So I take the problem to my corkboard and I do something crazy: I pull out a bunch of blank 3x5 cards and I start writing out tasks onto them:

- Run
- Groceries
- Pack for trip
- Monthly budget
- Writing project
- Email
- Lunch

Then I ask, for each one of these, will it take closer to thirty minutes, or an hour? If it's closer to thirty, I fold the 3x5 card in half.

So let's say it's 8:20 right now. I start by pinning my "Lunch" card in place at the 12:00 spot.

I also have a normal morning routine that I call my "boilerplate." Shower, shave, sync up my phone, etc. I can always knock that group of items out in about an hour. So I have a single 3x5 card for that, and I pin it to the board at the 8:30am spot.

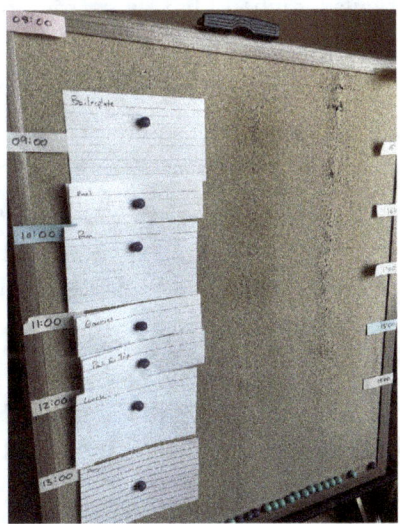

Going through my emails will take roughly thirty minutes. I fold that card in half and pin it up at the 9:30 spot.

Then I pin up my "Go for a run" card. That's close to an hour.

After that I can head to the grocery store and buy the five items I need for tonight's meal. That's a half hour.

I can also get most of my packing done for tomorrow's Chicago trip. That's a half hour as well.

There. That all gets me to my lunch time at 12:00 noon. My friend will be here at 1:00.

This is the perfect sanity check. My whole morning is right there, represented in physical space on the corkboard.

Sure, there's a bunch of other stuff I could try to get done this morning, but that's tossed for the time being. I know what I can do here, right now. I have the clarity I need. I can dive into it. It requires no further thought, and that's liberating.

To be clear, I do *not* do this every day. In fact, I never even do it for a single full day. It's only to get clarity on my next two or three hours. Particularly when I have a narrow time window with a hard stop approaching, and I need to be able to (literally) *see and feel* what I can and cannot finish between now and then.

It's an extra step, just in case, for those rare moments where things feel murky or I'm getting weirdly anxious about my time.

Plus I'm observing a larger The Art of Agile Living principle here: I can and will only ever do one thing at a time. I refuse to multitask. At any given moment I don't want to be thinking about anything other than the one item I'm working on right now.

With the corkboard trick, I know what I do and do not have time for. I've accounted for everything. It's visible. The cards serve as hard physical constraints that represent the time I need to do each task.

Now I can launch into the next few hours with zero distractions.

The Power of Pairing

Your Agile "workout buddy"

Kanban, as used in software development, was originally created as a team activity. It uses a group kanban board and all the familiar sticky notes. Tasks are broken down into small segments of two hours or less, just as we've discussed. The team gathers around the group kanban board, often labeled with the common "To Do", "Doing", and "Done" columns.

One of the great benefits of team kanban is transparency. Everyone in the group knows who is responsible for what, what each person is working on today, and what the status is for each item.

If a task isn't getting done, everybody knows it. This provides powerful motivation for each team member to complete their work on time.

The Art of Agile Living is different in that it's specific to your own individual workload. All the organizing benefits are there, of course; when you follow the steps, the process works, and it gives you feedback as you go.

If you want to stay motivated, stick to the process.

There is one thing that we've left unmentioned until now: the group element. With no team watching your progress, it might be easy to slip into procrastination. And that in turn affects not just you, but everyone in your circle who happens to be counting on you.

It turns out that 200,000 years of human evolution have taught us some vital lessons about staying motivated and happy in our work. I'll break it down for you into two major elements.

First Element: Keep it Physical

This book so far has described for you how to take abstract work and make it physical and concrete. The entire The Art of Agile Living process centers on physical things that you touch and move. These include:

- pens and pencils and colored markers
- tasks in the form of sticky notes
- separate sheets of paper that represent the days of the week and your backlog.

We've taught you about kinesthetics, which are essential to motivation:

- Working with actual pieces of paper fuels your motivation.
- Writing, handling, and moving notes fuels your motivation.
- Physically checking off finished tasks fuels your motivation.

The little endorphin rush you get as you complete each task is precisely what we're after.

There's a reason why we do *not* have you do this on a computer! Our human brains evolved to do physical work, to touch and move things in physical space. When we work this way we stay far more engaged.

Plus, when you keep everything physical and visible, you capture tasks you might otherwise miss. You prevent the chaos of last-minute rushes and unwanted all-nighters.

Second Element: Make it Social

As we've evolved to interact with a physical environment, we've also evolved for a *social* one.

To the degree that you're naturally fed by extrinsic motivators, to that degree you may be missing out on an additional powerful piece of motivation: the boost you get from other people.

To review: extrinsic motivation is where you get a reward by completing work for others. It's when having others depend on you is a strong positive driver.

Interacting socially provides a host of terrific extrinsic motivators.

If you've tried personal time management techniques and haven't been successful, you might need more than a book or a class. The single most powerful solution that we know of is to spend time each week doing The Art of Agile Living, in real time, *with others*. Find a partner and pair up. We've found that this works even if you and your partner are doing separate, unrelated projects.

Your Agile "Workout Buddy"

Some people are happy to go to the gym, exercise, and work out entirely on their own. If that's you, great. You can probably skip this social step, especially if your habit is to work out reliably by yourself at home.

But for many of us, having a workout buddy makes a world of difference. The Art of Agile Living works on this same principle.

To the degree that you benefit from having a workout buddy, to that same degree you will benefit from having an The Art of Agile Living buddy. Someone you "work out with," in a live meeting, at the same time at least once each week.

Anyone who can understand and follow this process—whether they're there in the room with you or a thousand miles away—can be your accountability partner. And you can be theirs.

Reach out and find a buddy, schedule a fixed time every week, and meet up live, either in person or on your favorite video conferencing platform.

Make your work visible: share your daily sheets, your backlog, your sticky notes, your time estimates. Arrange them right there, live, in real time, as your buddy watches and listens. And then have your buddy do the same for you.

Then watch your motivation soar.

Key Takeaways

- The Art of Agile Living is a wonderful way to manage your own work, but it also benefits from adding in team elements.
- If you've struggled with motivation, embrace the physical aspect that the process provides.
- If you still struggle, schedule a regular time every week to do The Art of Agile Living with a planning buddy.

Variations on a Theme: The Art of Agile Living for Family Get-Togethers

Engaging the entire family in preparing family events

I love family dinners, particularly special events like holiday meals. The camaraderie around a well-set and bountiful table, glistening with fine china and family silver; all the special treats for everyone, including two types of cranberry sauce.

When my family arrives for a big event or for the holidays, I'm always asked the same question. I imagine you're asked this too: "What can I do to help?"

In the past I often felt frazzled with this request, given all the things I was juggling in my head. I was already working to get the house in order and things ready—the table set, the silver out, drinks prepared, potatoes cooked and mashed, meat roasted and carved.

Sure, it would be nice to have help. But I never had a ready answer on the spot. So I'd just say "Oh, nothing. I've got it all handled. Have a seat and be comfortable."

As an Agilist, part of me knew this answer was crazy. I really could use the help. It would make all the preparations go smoother. And I knew that people genuinely enjoy being helpful; when they offer to pitch in, they mean it sincerely. I just had no easy way of making it happen.

Agile to the Rescue, Again

Then I attended a session at an Agile conference that changed everything. The central topic was getting groups of people to work together using kanban. The facilitator mentioned—almost in passing—how they use a kanban board for family meals.

My ears perked up. *Wait a minute, this is a real problem I have now!*

They described how they write out every task on a sticky note and publicly display it on their kitchen cabinet. Guests arrive for the meal, pick items off the board, and do them.

I was sold. I would try this at our next family meal. And I'd finally have an answer when people asked how they could help.

Christmas came and we invited the family for dinner. I prepared for their arrival: I wrote out a sticky note for every item I could think of that family members could help with. Tasks like setting the table, making coffee, mashing potatoes, and the like.

Each item needed to be clear enough to convey exactly what I needed done. So for example, instead of "Set the table," I created multiple stickies with specific instructions such as: "Put china plates on table", "Get silver out and put fork, knife, spoon at each place setting", "Fold and place napkins on table", "Put wine and water glasses on table", and "Get extra chairs from basement and place around table".

Put china plates on table	Get silver out and put fork, knife, spoon at each place setting	Fold and place napkins on table	Put wine and water glasses on table	Get extra chairs from basement and place around table

These sticky notes were placed on an ad-hoc Kanban board in my kitchen - on the sliding glass doors. With the columns labeled simply "To Do", "Doing", and "Done". My notes were specific and detailed enough that any person of any age or ability could read and take action on them. Sure, I had to point out where the silverware and fine china were kept. But once I did so, everyone knew where to find things and what to do, with no further direction from me.

On the very first try, it worked!

Family members arrived and asked the usual "What can I do to help?" question. I simply smiled, pointed at the kanban board, and said, "Pick one."

Variations on a Theme: The Art of Agile Living for Family Get-Togethers

With little additional input from me, all the tasks got done. I could now enjoy the family meal far more *because I wasn't doing everything*. Family members felt less like an imposition and more like active contributors.

And Then, a Surprise

Once I was willing to give up total control over every little detail, I reaped some unexpected rewards.

My daughter-in-law chose the sticky note that said "Fold and place napkins on table." She put her enthusiasm and creativity to work and made little Christmas trees from my napkins and napkin rings. How delightful! A beautiful piece of art for our holiday table—an end result better than anything I could have imagined.

Just as we promote self-organization and autonomy in our Agile teams, I discovered a clear application at home that rewarded creativity.

This is truly the spirit of The Art of Agile Living—timeless principles put to use in every department of your life.

And now when my family members arrive for a get-together, they don't even need to ask. They simply walk over to the kanban board, pick a task, and do it. When all the items are finished we remove the board from the wall and sit down to enjoy the meal.

I've used this method for everything from family dinners to graduation and engagement parties, all with the same level of success. Folks arrive, they chip in to help get things ready, and we all relax and enjoy each other's company.

Watch as the Idea Spreads

Last summer I visited my son and daughter-in-law at their new house. As new homeowners they had the usual long list of home repairs, minor fixes, and decorating tweaks that needed doing. But their DIY home repair skills were still in the "growing stage"—it was clear that they could use some help from Mom and Dad!

When we arrived we were greeted with a surprise: They had their very own kanban board on their kitchen glass door. The same open, visible location I like to use for my own lists.

And that's not all. Everything was broken down according to tasks for Dad and tasks for Mom. Some things my son and husband would work on, and others my daughter-in-law and I would tackle. These included things like:

- Fix bathroom towel bar
- Hang towel hooks in bathroom
- Cut cold air return vent into furnace
- Hang living room shelves
- Hang curtain rod over kitchen sliding door
- Shop for curtains for kitchen

During the day-long visit we paired off. We went shopping; we measured, drilled, and placed towel bars and hooks; we spackled; we hung curtain rods and curtains. We worked our way through the entire list, updating the kanban board with each completed task.

Having the items clearly identified and posted kept us focused and on track. My husband commented that by having the bigger picture available he felt like his time was respected. He could choose the order of his tasks and also plan for breaks and meals.

At the end of the day, we had completed every last item. We sat down for a nice family dinner ... with some well-deserved drinks!

With Agile, you know you've accomplished something special when you watch the process self-replicate. Seeing the kanban board there at my son and daughter-in-law's house was incredibly rewarding. It confirmed my belief that people genuinely want to be useful when they come to visit, and that having a list ready for them is both welcomed and welcoming.

Now it's your turn. Go to A2Agile.com/theartofagileliving[1], or email us at TheArtofAgileLiving@A2Agile.com, and tell us your own The Art of Agile Living story.

Key Takeaways

- At parties and gatherings, people find great satisfaction in helping.
- Kanban is the perfect tool for getting everyone involved.
- Post your "board" in an open, visible location where everyone can see and work with it.
- Write out individual tasks in clear, concise language.
- Give up control over small details and you'll see surprising creativity.

---

[1] http://A2Agile.com/theartofagileliving

- You'll know you've done something truly special when you see others replicate your method.

The Doorway Effect

How walking through doorways dumps your short term memory and what to do about it

I was recently in my bedroom hanging some clothes when I spotted a piece of string that needed cutting off a blouse. The scissors were in the kitchen, so I headed out the bedroom door and down the hallway to retrieve them. As I entered the kitchen I wandered aimlessly for a second or two, then noticed the dishwasher needed emptying, so I did that immediately.

I had forgotten why I came to the kitchen in the first place.

I wandered back to my bedroom and suddenly remembered why I had gone to the kitchen. Heading out the door a second time to get the scissors, the same thing happened again.

This time I ended up vacuuming.

Wherever I share this experience, people relate. And they tell me similar stories of their own. It turns out this phenomenon is so common that researchers took up the formal study of it and gave it a name: the Doorway Effect[1].

The scientific theory goes something like this: part of our short-term memory is dependent on context. When we have the intention of going to the kitchen to fetch a pair of scissors, that gets stored in a memory package along with present-moment contextual details such as our physical location—in this case, the bedroom.

---

[1] https://www.scientificamerican.com/article/why-walking-through-doorway-makes-you-forget/

But that memory package can be fickle. The moment we get up, walk through a doorway, and change our visual context—researchers have found—we dump as much as 25% of our short-term memory.

In short: Walk through a door, dump your memory.

From an evolutionary point of view, we can guess why this would be true. Walk out of a forest and into an open meadow and your brain now has to deal with new context. Are there snakes? or predators? Is there food to be had? Your brain has only so much memory space to work with, so it files away the old forest data and makes room for the new meadow context.

This is Virtual, Too

Pause and reflect on this for a moment: Changes in what you are seeing in your environment can cause you to forget your intentions.

But it gets more interesting. The researchers who studied the Doorway Effect asked another question: For those of us using a computer, does walking through a *virtual* doorway do the same thing? If you go through a door in a video game like World of Warcraft, do you dump part of your short-term memory?

Great question. Would you care to guess the answer?

It turns out we do. A doorway in a video game can trigger your brain to dump memory just like a real physical door.

And that's not all. Other aspects of an onscreen user interface behave just like a virtual doorway. Have you ever been on a computer and lost track of a task as soon as you opened a new window or tab, or a popup dinged at you? Near as I can tell, everyone has.

Most people I've talked to over the years were unaware of the Doorway Effect until I pointed it out. But once you see it, you can't unsee it.

Your Computer is a Culprit

If you use your computer, phone, or tablet to manage your tasks, unlike with the physical The Art of Agile Living paper system we teach, *the very act of managing those tasks is likely causing you to lose focus.* Each time you switch to a new window or open a separate application to write down an idea for a task, the software itself triggers your brain to snuff out the idea and dump your memory, and your intentions along with it.

It's bad enough when this happens to you at home as you're thinking about a pair of scissors. But if your task management software is doing this to you, that's borderline criminal.

Every kind of software I regularly encounter does this. It places virtual doors everywhere in your path. Windows open and close. *Your intentions get dumped.* Apps pop up in the foreground. A new shopping cart tab opens. *More of your memory, dumped.*

I no longer blame myself for forgetting things when I walk through doorways, real or virtual. It's simply how our human brain works. But I do blame software designers. Both Microsoft and Apple operating systems actively and constantly push us through virtual doors. User-interface designers, advertisers, marketers ... even Agile task-tracking software products trigger us to dump our short-term memory.

This only adds obstacles to managing our work well.

Stickies, Everywhere

Even the The Art of Agile Living paper system is subject to this issue. After all, we each have homes with rooms and doorways! But there's a simple strategy to deal with this.

Remember how I said that I keep sticky pads all over the house? This is why. When an idea comes to me, I write it on a note before I leave the room. I take it with me through the door, and now I have a way to remember what I would otherwise forget.

Keep it Physical, Keep it Safe

Our process helps with this, by design. Virtual windows on your computer open and close all the time, but the The Art of Agile Living daily task sheet sitting on your physical desktop does not. It stays there as an anchor to permanent reality. So long as it's visible in front of you, it will be impervious to the Doorway Effect.

Agile folks like me have been observing the Doorway Effect for years. After all, we make it our job to notice how work feels and how our minds and bodies respond when doing tasks. This is why we love using physical boards located on physical walls where we can see and track everything we do.

Now that you have a name for the Doorway Effect, say it out loud a few times. Grab a sticky note and write it down, now, before you leave the room you're in. In fact, do it before you close this book … or the virtual window where you're currently reading it!

All of this is yet another excellent reason to follow the The Art of Agile Living process exactly as described in this book. When you keep your task set physical—and keep it there in the room with you—you don't forget it.

Key Takeaways

- Any time you walk through a doorway, you dump part of your short term memory.
- This is true of virtual interfaces. With digital devices, you continually expose yourself to the Doorway Effect.
- To bypass this problem, use physical sheets of paper for your The Art of Agile Living work and keep today's sheet visible.
- Keep sticky notes in every room of your house and write down your ideas as they come. That ensures they'll survive the Doorway Effect.

The Checklist and the Ceremony

The Art of Agile Living is not a checklist, it's a ceremony

Every year my husband and I visit the Yankee air museum in Belleville, Michigan. We're members and we love it. We go to see some of its most iconic aircraft fly, especially the Boeing B-17 Flying Fortress.

When a B-17's engines start, the earth shakes and you feel it all around you. You can't help but be transported back to a dramatic and terrifying chapter in American History, World War II.

The story of this amazing machine has a special relevance to the themes in this book.

With war in Europe looming, the B-17 had a rocky start as an experimental aircraft. On October 20, 1935, during a key demonstration test flight in Ohio for the Army Air Corps, the plane stalled, crashed, and burst into flames. The entire crew was killed.

Perhaps the aircraft was "too much plane for one man to fly," as one local paper reported. Some claimed it had too many switches, as the crash had been caused by one single switch incorrectly set.

If the Boeing Corporation, who designed the B-17, was going to win the contract as a primary supplier for the U.S. military, they had a major problem to solve: how young, freshly trained pilots could reliably set all the switches into all the right positions for all the various tasks necessary for startup, takeoff, flying, bombing, landing, and shutdown.

Enter the Checklist

Check Lists In Cockpit

EVERY AIRPLANE HAS CHECK LISTS PROVIDED FOR THE FOLLOWING:

1. Before starting engine or engines.
2. During warm-up.
3. Before takeoff.
4. During flight.
5. Before landing.
6. After landing.

As the story is traditionally told, Boeing solved the problem by creating checklists. A checklist for before starting the engine, a checklist during warm-up, a checklist before takeoff, a checklist during flight, before and after landing. They printed and placed in the cockpit a list that covered every step in the flight sequence. The pilot and copilot together would systematically go over each item on the list—every dial, every setting, every switch. Crews were trained to follow the checklists and ensure that the plane was always ready for each stage of flight.

The checklists worked, according to the story. The B-17 flew. The Allies won the war. The free world was saved.

After the war, the idea caught on and spread. Checklists were now seen as the answer to every management problem, every technical issue, every project, every complex task, regardless of the industry.

"This is how humans are going to manage complexity in the modern age!" we were told. Checklists were a panacea, applied to every situation whether appropriate or not.

Eventually this emerged in its most egregious form of all: checklists for creating checklists covering things like the font type and size, use of TLAs[1], whether others were consulted in creating the checklist, and so on.

CHECKLIST FOR CHECKLISTS

Development
- [ ] Do you have a vague idea for a checklist?

    Is each item?
- [ ] Arcane
- [ ] Boring
- [ ] Tedious
- [ ] Painful

    Have you considered?
- [ ] Making communication as obtuse as possible?
- [ ] Ignoring others while building your checklist?

Drafting
- [ ] Does the Checklist?
- [ ] Breakup the natural flow of work?
- [ ] Use complex and obscure language?
- [ ] Contain lots of TLAs?
- [ ] Maximize the use of color?

    Is the Font?
- [ ] Comic sans?
- [ ] Too small to read comfortably?
- [ ] Is the date of creation hidden or unclear?

Validation

    Have You?
- [ ] Launched the Checklist with no testing?
- [ ] Aggressive avoided helpful feedback?

    Does the Checklist?
- [ ] Break the flow of work?
- [ ] Correctly detect errors too late?
- [ ] Take way too much time and energy?
- [ ] Result in emotional damage to the user?
- [ ] Have a way to live forevever without question?

Without a Ceremony, It's Useless

There's a fundamental problem with this entire narrative. What saved the B-17 and the Boeing Corporation—and ultimately the free world—was not a checklist.

What saved it was a ritual. A *ceremony*.

The checklist was merely a tool, a physical object around which the larger ceremony was built.

---

[1]TLA stands for Three Letter Acronyms, those little code words that have become the bane of clear communication for so many of us.

The pilot and copilot picked up and handled the list. They verbally called out each item on it. They physically touched each switch and with their fingers they moved it to its correct position. They called back and forth to confirm that each item was completed. This was a very physical process.

The Crucial Mistake

Seeing only checklists and missing the larger context and physical structure around the B-17 ceremony was a mistake. A huge mistake.

As a result, checklists for so many people nowadays have been reduced to meaningless paperwork, to long, tedious forms—an enormous joy-killing nuisance.

The Art of Agile Living is sometimes mistakenly compared to creating checklists. Sure, it has a number of checklist elements. In my case, I do in fact put a checkmark on each sticky note when I move it to the done side of the page.

But the power of The Art of Agile Living goes far beyond simply checking off items. It's a *ceremonial* way to approach your work, whether you do it alone or with others.

Don't get me wrong: Documenting a procedure for how to review the switches in a B-17 was essential. Having a checklist for exactly how each switch was to be set was indispensable. But it was *the cockpit ceremony*—with pilot and copilot working together to physically review the checklist—that saved lives and ensured the success of the entire operation.

Without the ceremony, the system fails.

As we said at the very beginning, this book is not about tasks, sticky notes, or sheets of papers. And it's not about checklists. It's about creating a ritual for structuring and planning your day, a ceremony that becomes so much of a habit, so much of a pleasure, that *you're no longer comfortable starting your day without it.*

Bring on the Copilot!

And yet to truly leverage the power of this ritual, there's a key secret we haven't addressed, a secret revealed in the B-17 story: doing the ceremony with another person, a copilot.

Tom and I have been running an Agile consulting business for years. There was a stretch of time where we worked in the same office and, not surprisingly, we did all of our planning using the Agile method. Kanban, the sticky notes, the sheets, everything. And we did it at the same time every day.

The key was that we did it together, just like the pilot and copilot in an airplane cockpit. There were specific items Tom was doing, other items I was doing, plus all of the things we were working on jointly. Whatever the tasks, we talked through them every day, calling out each specific item, together, as a pair.

As we've shown you throughout this book, The Art of Agile Living is a powerful method for tracking and sharing personal work. But it's more than that. It's a way of having productive ritualized formal conversations with others. It's asking,

- What is the work we're doing?
- Should we do this item?
- Do we really need to do that item?
- Who should be doing what?
- What does it mean for this task to be done?

That's what Agile is about. That's the complete picture.

Choose NOT to Do It

Two of the most powerful decisions in The Art of Agile Living work are often best made with other people: specifically, choosing to give a task to someone else, and choosing not to do a task at all.

The human brain is a wonderful thing. Give it a little time and it will be an endless source of ideas, tasks, and inspirations. (And sticky notes!) However, just because your brain came up with an idea—and you wrote it down—does not mean the idea is good. And even if it is the right idea, neither does it mean that it's something you yourself should actually do.

There will always be tasks where you repeatedly find yourself pulling the note off today's page and sticking it onto tomorrow's sheet. Or worse, you wrote it down and put it on your backlog sheet but it never gets moved, never gets scheduled into an actual day's work.

This is where doing the daily ceremony with your copilot can be invaluable.

On your own, it's hard to give up tasks you've written down. You own the thing; you want to see it done ... or so you think. But if it never gets completed—and maybe never even gets scheduled—that says something.

Your copilot doesn't own the item; they're not attached to it. They'll always be far more willing to ask, "Is this *really* something you want to do?"

Remember the Princess, from the parable. Recall how at the end of the story she had to be reminded by the others that she had once wished for a hippopotamus. She recognized at that moment that she didn't need one after all.

Always be hippo hunting. Working with your copilot, be in the regular habit of throwing out old unfinished tasks that upon further reflection are just not essential.

Choose to Hand it Off

Your copilot can also help you with a second decision: the choice to hand off the task to someone else.

Let's say your original inspiration about a particular task was right. It's a good idea and it needs to be done, but you've never gotten around to scheduling it.

There's a lot you can learn from this. Try giving the task to someone else. Your copilot can be especially helpful because they can either take on the task themself or they can recommend someone else who can do it. Either way, the second pair of eyes gives you invaluable perspective.

The Art of Agile Living is powerful all by itself—just you, following the process. But it is *most powerful* when done with coworkers, loved ones, or friends.

Key Takeaways

- The Art of Agile Living is not a checklist, it's a ceremony.
- Checklists may be useful but they're only a piece of a larger process for managing projects.
- Invite a copilot to join you in your The Art of Agile Living ceremony.
- Have your copilot help you make your two biggest "not to do" decisions: identifying hippos, and handing tasks off to others.

A Day in the Life

Using the process on a daily basis

It's early evening on Sunday. I walk over to my planning sheets and folder and first review the weekend's activities. I look at what may not have been finished, and do my retrospective. Asking myself what was about those particular tasks that I could not finish them, or in some cases, even start them? What about the tasks that did get completed, why were those possible to finish?

This is the same retrospective that I do daily. Asking myself if the most important tasks got done, what were the easiest tasks, and what were the hardest ones? Then asking myself what about those easy tasks made them easy? What about the hard ones made them so difficult to get completed? I often find that keeping the tasks small makes a difference. A big difference. Smaller tasks are easier to get accomplished. They take less time, are more focused, and have a clear definition of what I consider 'Done' to mean.

Defining Done

It can be rather easy to write up a sticky note for something like 'make sure I have enough money to retire'. On the surface that sounds reasonable. But is this something I can actually work on? What does it enough money mean? How do I find out what I need? How do I actually go about ensuring I will have this amount when I'm ready to retire?

When I start to think about this, I realize it is more of a goal than a task. What would I consider to be 'done' for this task? When I begin to think about this task in terms of 'done', it starts to break down into a number of activities, possibly something like this:

- Research financial advisors in my area, ask friends and family for recommendations
- Interview financial advisors
- Select financial advisor
- Determine how much money I will need to retire with financial advisor
- Develop an investment plan with financial advisor
- Establish an investment plan with financial advisor
- Evaluate current 401k contributions and adjust as needed for my investment plan
- Set up an IRA with financial advisor
- Contribute to IRA
- Set up annual plan for IRA contributions

Each of these activities are focused on one specific task. Each of these has a clear definition of done. It is these focused, and smaller tasks that lend themselves to getting done. I won't argue that some of these might still feel big, such as setting up an investment plan with a financial advisor. Likely this one gets further broken down into a number of smaller tasks as I work with the financial advisor.

This list of tasks is my starting point. Something far more workable than simply 'Make sure I have enough money to retire'.

Think small. Get focused. Write lots of sticky notes.

Those Unfinished Tasks

Despite our best attempts at making tasks small, keeping them focused, and defining done, there may still be things that don't get completed as planned. It is a natural approach to simply move the task forward to my weekly planning sheets, perhaps directly to Monday. But this is a dangerous approach. It can lead to a task getting moved forward day after day after day without ever getting done. At the time a task is not completed is the time to review it and ask yourself 'should this be carried forward to the upcoming week, should it be moved to the backlog, or should it be done at all?'.

If it should be carried forward, I'll pull it off the Weekend planning sheet and put in on my desk. In a moment I'll decide where best to place it. I don't automatically move it to a specific day.

If this task should be moved back to the backlog, I'll put it there. Perhaps it is not a time critical task, something that could be done at a later time.

If this task should not be done at all, I crumple it up and toss it in the trash. Oh what a wonderful feeling! One less thing that I need to do. It is entirely possible that the task was once a good idea, but circumstances have changed such that the task is no longer needed. You might remember this from our 'Review Your Day' chapter as being a 'hippo'[1]. Yes, those tasks that sounded good at the time, but no longer need to be worked on at all. This is where we continue our 'hippo hunting'. We do it daily. We do it weekly during our

---

[1] From the book *The Scrum Princess* by Kyle and Demi Aretae, https://thescrumprincess.com.

weekend planning for the upcoming week. We're always on the hunt for hippos.

I pull out my Backlog sheet and review it. Generally it is in an order of importance, with the items on the top left being the ones most likely to be done next. I'll identify which of those items are appropriate for this upcoming week. Those get put on the desk. I get a nice little pile of items on my desk for the next weeks planning.

Next I pull up my electronic calendar. I'm looking for meetings and appointments that are demands on my time, making sure there is a sticky note for each one with its requisite estimation. I'll write sticky notes for those items, and since they came from my calendar, I already know the precise day and time they occur. I'll put the time of the event in the upper left corner of the sticky note, and the time estimate on the lower right corner. I then put these sticky notes on the planning sheet for the day and time they are to occur. I do this for EVERY demand on my time. Meetings. Appointments. Picking up the kids from day care. Lately I have been including sticky notes for any planned breaks, such as the afternoon coffee break that my husband and I take every day around 3 pm. It's a great break to catch up on some reading, or just unplug for a short bit to recharge our batteries. It is a demand on my time, and if I'm going to take that break every day, I had better include it on my planning sheet.

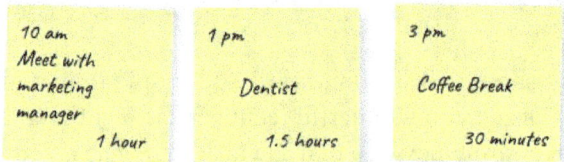

Next I take that nice little pile of sticky notes that I pulled from the backlog and begin to place them on my planning sheets. For each task, determining which day is appropriate for each task. I'll also take the time to write up new sticky notes for items that may have come up recently. These get placed on the planning sheets as well.

I now have a draft plan for my upcoming week. I know what is coming up for Monday. Having the appointments and meetings on the planning sheets also gives me a great view of what the week will look like. It lets me prepare a bit mentally for it. And for which tasks are scheduled to get done.

My Daily Ceremony

Before breakfast I take a quick look at my planning sheet for today. Just in case there is something early on my schedule that I placed there likely less than a week ago. A lot may have happened since then, even since last night, and I may have forgotten about this early commitment. When I don't check my planning sheet before breakfast, that's when I'm most likely to miss something important.

Once I'm ready to start my day, I take my planning sheet folder and place it with the current day's planning sheet face up and on top of the pile of planning sheets. I now have today's activities laid out in front of me on my desk. I have clarity and focus on my work. I begin work on the top item on my planning sheet.

I continue to work on the tasks as they were placed on my planning sheet. However, it is very likely that something unexpected will come up. I'll get asked by a colleague to do something for them. Or my manager will ask for an impromptu meeting. Or maybe there's a call from one of my children asking for help with something. Or an email that needs immediate attention. There can be a myriad of things that come up during our days to derail our best laid plans. This is precisely why we don't schedule more than 6 hours of activities in a work day. Unexpected things happen.

Dealing with Interrupts

I write up a sticky note for each of the newly identified tasks that will need to be done either today, this week, or at some point in the future. Some people like to use a specific color to identify interrupt tasks. You may want to pick a sticky note color that is unique to interrupt tasks. If you get a lot of interrupts, this can be a wonderful visualization of how interrupt driven your day is. Having this information lets you begin the process of identifying what can be done about it. Such as asking if there is there someone else that can handle some of these interrupts. Or looking deeper as to why these interrupts are happening at all. Asking yourself, and perhaps others, if there is there a process improvement that would alleviate these interrupts? Or perhaps you adjust downward your daily productive time from 6 hours to something less. The terrific benefit is that you know how much time you truly have available for task work in your day. This is a big help in avoiding overscheduling your day and therefore reducing your overwhelm.

Next I estimate the task. I ask of the requestor when this task needs to be done, and if today is already fully booked, can this task be completed another day? I'll even ask if I have to do the task, or can someone else.

Next I place the task appropriately on one of the planning sheets. It's either on another day's sheet, the backlog sheet, or today's sheet. If it's on today's sheet, I need to identify what other task or tasks are to be removed to make room for this new interrupt task. If the requestor is also a requestor of one of the other tasks on my daily sheet, I show them my planning sheet - all laid out with today's demands on my time and scheduled tasks, and ask them which of the two they requested of me is to be done today.

This is another great benefit of using the Art of Agile Living planning sheets. Other people can see clearly what your day looks like, and what demands you already have on your time. It is there in black and white (and some lively color if you are so inclined). You can have meaningful conversations about the demands on your time. Perhaps they see that you are attending a meeting that day that they can attend in your place. Perhaps there is another task that they agree can be done by someone else. Maybe even them!

The visibility of your work is a powerful resource. Be ready to share it with others. Walk them through your day. You'll be surprised on how this changes the conversation from 'just get it done' to something far more meaningful about the demands on your time and the work you are doing.

The rest of the day continues in the similar fashion. Once the top item is completed, and I've put that satisfying check mark on it and moved it to the DONE column, I'll pull up the next task and place it at the top left of the planning sheet. And so it goes until the day is done. Each time an interrupt occurs, I follow the same procedure as outlined above. Each time the day's plan may get adjusted. Each time it is a conscious and intentional adjustment.

Daily Retrospective

At the end of the day, usually sometime in the evening, I review my planning sheet and hold my daily retrospective. Just like what I described at the beginning of this chapter for the weekend review. What did not get done today? Why do I feel that was? Does the task need to be carried forward to the next day, or should this be rescheduled to another day, or moved to the backlog? Or better yet, should this task be completed at all?

The daily retrospective is designed to probe what motivates me. I'll ask myself, was the task too large, or too ill-defined for me to want to work on it? Does the task feel more like drudgery than something interesting? Is there a way to redefine the task so it is more appealing for me to work on it? I'll take the time to rewrite the task as appropriate. Likely the estimate will change with a rewrite. Hopefully the estimate is now shorter. Shorter tasks are always easier for me to get done. Even the tasks that feel like drudgery.

My planning sheets for the remainder of the week may change based on the outcomes from my daily retrospective. I make that change now. And I review what is on tomorrow's schedule. What is happening first, when do I have availability, what kind of day will tomorrow feel like. I can now get ready for settling down for the evening knowing that my schedule is under control, and knowing what is to be expected of me for the next day.

Key takeaways:

- Start each day with a quick review of the schedule
- Write up a sticky note for each interrupt task
- Visualization of your work enables meaningful discussions with colleagues
- Daily retrospectives foster better tasks

In Closing: A Solution You Can Stick With

Building the daily and weekly rhythms that ensure adherence to The Art of Agile Living

I've been using this method in some form or another since 2007. Some days I feel like I'm single-handedly keeping the 3M Company afloat with all my sticky notes! And yet the process has been my constant companion, through work commitments, holiday plans, graduations, engagement parties, weddings, and more. Even better, I've watched my method get picked up and embraced by family and friends.

I know the system works. And yet sticking to a new process is not always easy at first.

Those Old Abandoned Methods

All my previous attempts at planning sit like relics in a museum case. My old Franklin Planner binder is now repurposed as an ordinary notebook. Old list pads and pamphlets get used as scrap paper. Boxes of filing cards pepper my bookshelves as unintentional bookends. The electrons of old Trello boards wither away in the cloud. And then there are all those endless checklists.

Don't get me wrong—I love checklists. They serve a strong, if limited, purpose. I rely on checklists for sets of tasks that are fairly static and repeatable. For example, I manage our annual winter treks to Florida with detailed checklists on what to pack and how to prepare the house for a multi-month departure. These are more or less the same each year: turn off the water; forward the mail; turn the heat down, and more. Checklists are great for this.

But none of those old time- and task-management methods ever ultimately did the trick for me. One by one I abandoned each of them. And it wasn't for lack of desire to succeed. Rather, it was the way that these methods left me so completely disengaged from my immediate physical world.

The Art of Agile Living reverses that. It's not cerebral; it's kinesthetic. It puts a pen and paper back in your hand. It keeps you active with sticky notes and a simple folder. It provides you with a ceremonial physical action for each task you complete. It takes the abstract and makes it concrete again; it puts you and your work back in step with your physical surroundings.

Designed to Help You Stick to It

And there's more. Built into the practice are simple methods to help you maintain it:

- It allows you time every day to review what got done.
- You give yourself daily feedback on what you liked and what you didn't.
- A simple Monday session lets you plan out your entire week.
- Your backlog sheet is always a perfect storage spot for your longer-range items.
- The 7-Sheet Plan gives you a place to track every task, every idea that comes up.
- With your folder, everything stays cleanly out of sight except your items for today.

The system is made to be flexible. When unexpected things inevitably pop up, you'll be able to move items around, adjust your priorities, change the sequence of your tasks, and postpone things where necessary. And spotting and getting rid of hippos is easy.

With everything in your week accounted for, you're free to focus exclusively on what needs to be done right now.

You'll love the rhythms. Your daily and weekly reviews will become a familiar beat. Everything can coalesce into an embedded practice. As with any new process, the more you do it, the easier and more natural it will feel.

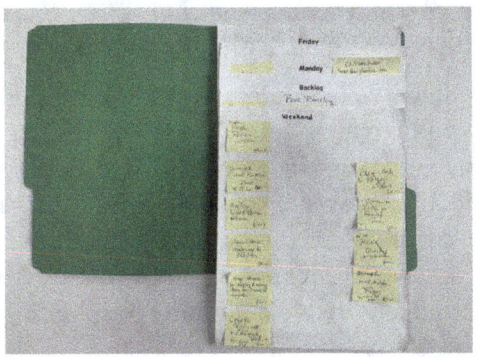

You CAN Take it With You

You're also now armed with a simple tool: a file folder with a sheet for today on top. You can literally take this with you wherever you move about, whether your home office, your kitchen, your workshop, your studio, or your outside office. Having it all at your fingertips keeps the process front and center, regardless of your location.

Best of all, your work area stays free of clutter. An entire week's plans take up barely more surface area than a single sheet of paper. It's well worth the use of desktop real estate to see your work accomplished.

All the Right Motivators

My personality is such that I can maintain this process without extrinsic motivators. Tom is different; he benefits from doing his structured planning sessions with a partner. So he and I schedule a weekly meetup to go through our joint work and our individual personal tasks. The regular, structured session gives him the motivation he needs to stick with the process.

The lesson here? Understand what motivates you most, and use the approach that best aligns with you.

If you enjoy joint weekly planning sessions, find a buddy — someone who will keep you zeroed in on your daily priorities. This can be a significant other, a work colleague, a close friend, a family member. Build in a little bit of social time into your session as well. And if for each weekly meetup you can reciprocate, walking your buddy through his or her plans too, all the better. Mutual support and shared accountability are a winning formula.

Over the years, I've found this to be a process I can stick with. As a result I've maintained a reliable exercise regimen, managed residences and property in two different states, run a consulting business, done home improvement projects with family, entertained guests at parties and holiday events, and written a book, all the while avoiding last minute panics and rushes ... and still reliably enjoying a good night's sleep.

With The Art of Agile Living, this can be your success story too!

Key Takeaways

- Take advantage of all the physical The Art of Agile Living structures and methods that help you stick with the process.
- Feel free to adapt when unexpected items and obligations come up.

- Enjoy the familiar rhythm of the daily and weekly reviews.
- Take your folder with you as you move about throughout the day.
- If you enjoy joint planning sessions, find a buddy to do it with you.

Resources

How overwhelmed are you? Get your **Overwhelm Score** at OverwhelmScore.com[1].

To learn about our program that teaches The Art of Agile Living™ in depth, visit: *https://www.a2agile.com/agile-at-home-program*[2].

To read more about the perils of multitasking:

Multitasking Can Make You Lose ... Um ... Focus[3]

Media multiskaters pay mental price, Stanford study shows[4]

To read further about different styles of learning:

Shaughnessy, M. F. (1998, January). An interview with Rita Dunn about learning styles. Clearing House, (71)3, (OCLC FirstSearchResources: Full Text)

To read more about the history of kinsethetics:

"The Sixth Sense": Towards a History of Muscular Sensation, by Roger Smith, Gesnerus 68/1 (2011) 218–71

To read more about innovative applications of The Art of Agile Living™: *https://www.slideshare.net/agileee/henrik-kniberg-agile-at-home*[5]

Some of the books that inspire our Agile approach include:

- *Ceremony: A Profound New Method for Achieving Successful and Sustainable Change* by Thomas Meloche
- *Joy, Inc.* by Richard Sheridan

---

[1] http://www.overwhelmscore.com
[2] https://www.a2agile.com/agile-at-home-program
[3] https://www.nytimes.com/2008/10/25/business/yourmoney/25shortcuts.html
[4] https://news.stanford.edu/2009/08/24/multitask-research-study-082409/
[5] https://www.slideshare.net/agileee/henrik-kniberg-agile-at-home

- *The Scrum Princess* by Kyle and Demi Aretae
- *The Scrum Guide* by Ken Schwaber & Jeff Sutherland
- *The People's Scrum* by Tobias Mayer
- *Scrum: The Art of Doing Twice the Work in Half the Time* by Jeff Sutherland
- *The Kanban Guide* at KanbanGuides.org
- *The Four Tendencies: The Indispensable Personality Profiles That Reveal How to Make Your Life Better (and Other People's Lives Better, Too)* by Gretchin Rubin
- *The Goal* by Eliyahu M. Goldratt
- *The Theory of Constraints* by Eliyahu M. Goldratt
- *Clean Language, Revealing Metaphors and Opening Minds* by Wendy Sullivan and Judy Rees

We'd love to hear from you! Try out The Art of Agile Living and visit *A2Agile.com/TheArtofAgileLiving*[6], or email us at *TheArtofAgileLiving@A2Agile.com*[7], and tell us your own The Art of Agile Living story.

---

[6] http://www.a2agile.com/TheArtofAgileLiving
[7] mailto:TheArtofAgileLiving@A2Agile.com

Acknowledgements

Helene's Acknowledgements

I want to thank LeanPub for providing a platform for authors. This delivery platform has enabled me to build a following, continuously deliver updated versions of the book, and feel very empowered as an author.

Heartfelt thanks to our Literary Advisor & Content Coach, John Willig, of Literary Services Inc. for all his insights and help in getting us to this point, and his diligence in navigating the publishing process. His belief in us and our materials has been a guiding force for our journey into publishing.

To my husband and best friend, David Gidley, whose consistent encouragement, insights, and support has been invaluable to not only my journey in completing this book, but in my life's journey.

A special thanks to my business partner, Thomas Meloche, for his encouragement and belief in this process and insightful contributions on content. It was his suggestion that I take this process that has been my guiding light for over twenty years and turn it into a book.

Many thanks to Bryan Todd for his outstanding editorial contributions to our book. His skilled editing not only proved instrumental in enhancing the overall quality but also enriched the content with valuable additions. His dedication, expertise, and enthusiasm are greatly appreciated.

A special thanks to Dr. Mari Kira, Assistant Professor of Psychology at the University of Michigan for her insights, suggestions, and continued support in my journey. A great friend, co-presenter at

Agile conferences, and second parent to our cat Stella, she has been a welcome force in my life.

Special thanks to Rich Sheridan, CEO Menlo Innovations and author of Joy, Inc. - How We Built a Workplace People Love and of Chief Joy Officer - How Great Leaders Elevate Human Energy and Eliminate Fear not only for his insightful comments on our book but for building a workplace that inspired me in more ways than I can count.

To our designer, Clara Trent, who helped design the book cover, your insights and designs made the book look its best. Thank you for your patience in working with us and keeping a sense of joy and fun throughout the process.

Many thanks to all those who helped review this book prior to this point and provided invaluable insights for us. We couldn't have done this without your help: Matt Lasater, Gabe Bautista, Mike Russell, Ron Jeffries, Bella St. John, Krista Van Prooyen, Bethany Meloche, Holly Bielawa, Megan Torrance.

Tom's Acknowledgements

In creating this book, I have been fortunate to work alongside Helene Gidley, a co-author whose vision and drive are surpassed only by her exceptional skills in daily time management. Helene embodies the principles of "The Art of Agile Living" — not just in theory, but as a practical, lived reality. Her dedication and insight have been crucial to transforming our ideas into the words that fill these pages. For her relentless commitment and inspiring ethos, I am profoundly grateful. Thank you, Helene, for making this journey not only possible but also a truly enriching experience.

About The Authors

Helene Gidley, a distinguished leader in the Agile community, has made a significant impact on the IT industry through her pioneering work with A2Agile Inc., a company she co-founded. As an accomplished Agile trainer, mentor, and coach, Helene has assisted a myriad of organizations in optimizing their Agile practices and attaining exceptional results. Her vast experience, spanning over thirty years, encompasses working with professionals from Fortune 500 companies, startups, and mid-sized organizations.

With over 15 years of experience as a certified Project Management Professional, Helene has expertly integrated the finest Project Management practices with Agile principles. Her innovative approach has gained widespread recognition, attracting an international audience to her annual Agile Coach Retreat, where she imparts her knowledge with fellow coaches from around the world.

Helene's dedication to supporting Agile growth in the community inspired her to establish the Agile Groupies Meetup in 2008. Based in Ann Arbor, Michigan, this thriving group meets regularly to collaborate to learn and enhance their Agile practices. As an esteemed speaker, Helene has engaged audiences at over 100 Meetups, Agile conferences, and Project Management Institute Chapter meetings.

In her spare time you'll find Helene busy biking, going on long walks with her husband David, and coddling her cat Stella.

Thomas Meloche is an accomplished marketing expert, best-selling author, and agile transformation leader with a proven track record of successfully launching and promoting products across various industries. With more than twenty-five years of experience, Thomas has demonstrated a unique ability to combine his deep knowledge of marketing strategies with agile methodologies to help organizations achieve remarkable results. Thomas' marketing prowess and extensive experience in the software startup industry make him the ideal candidate to promote and sell his new book to entrepreneurs and busy business professionals.

Thomas began his career as a software developer, which allowed him to gain invaluable hands-on experience in the technology industry. Over time, Thomas honed his marketing skills and co-founded Menlo Innovations LLC, one of the most successful agile software development houses in the United States. Menlo Innovations has been featured in the book "Joy Inc.: How We Built a Workplace People Love," which highlights the company's unique agile process, The Menlo Way, for rapidly producing high-quality software. Thousands of people visit Menlo from around the world every year to experience The Menlo Way firsthand.

As a marketing expert, Thomas has had a major impact on the industry through his best-selling book series, "Ultimate Guide to Facebook Advertising." Published by Entrepreneur Press, this series has provided businesses with invaluable insights and strategies for maximizing their marketing efforts on the Facebook platform. Thomas' success with this book series is a testament to his marketing abilities and his capacity to create compelling, informative content that resonates with readers.

In addition to his work at Menlo Innovations, Thomas has provided marketing consulting services through Perry Marshall and Associates since January 2011. In this role, Thomas has been instrumental in creating agile marketing and advertising teams for clients across various industries. His unique approach to marketing has produced significant results for his clients and further solidified his reputation as a top marketing expert.

Thomas' expertise in marketing is complemented by his extensive background in agile transformation. He has coached agile initiatives and transformed products, departments, and companies for over two decades. Thomas has worked with organizations of all sizes, ranging from Interface Systems with one team to USAA with 400 teams and a yearly development budget of 4.5 billion dollars.

Bryan Todd is a writer and marketing specialist in Lincoln, Nebraska. He's worked in North America, Europe, and Asia and has spent most of his career teaching—from foreign languages and world history to advanced testing methods for the internet, and even to self-help and theology. He helps people find their unique voice. He's worked with clients in dozens of industries from health care and book publishing to manufacturing and computer software.

www.ingramcontent.com/pod-product-compliance
Lightning Source LLC
Chambersburg PA
CBHW071053240526
45471CB00015B/1790